HUNTING WILD BOAR IN CALIFORNIA

by Bob Robb

ISBN 0-936513-09-8

Library of Congress 89-92684

Published by:

LARSEN'S OUTDOOR PUBLISHING
2640 Elizabeth Place
Lakeland, FL 33813

Distributed by:
Bob Robb
P.O. Box 1296
Valdez, AK 99686

PRINTED IN THE UNITED STATES OF AMERICA

4 5 6 7 8 9 10

DEDICATION

To my parents, Paul and Joanne Robb, who have supported me in all my ventures, from childhood to adulthood, no matter how crazy they have been, and who taught me early on that man hath no greater friend than Mother Nature.

ACKNOWLEDGEMENTS

Hunting hogs over the years has provided me with some of the most enjoyable and memorable days I've spent outdoors. My number one hog hunting buddy, Durwood Hollis, both encouraged and helped me no end with this project. We've shared lots of laughs, sweat, and hard work over the years, and for those I'll always be grateful, even though in the process he also gave a new meaning to the term, "Death March." Several guides and ranch owners have also been more than tolerant in permitting me to hunt and photograph hogs with them, and who also became my friends as well. To Mike Ballew, Wayne Long, Chuck Harrison, Craig Rossier, Mitch Roth, and Cliff & Darla Sebasto, thanks for your time and patience.

Thanks also go out to Jim Matthews for the use of his cover photograph, and for the friendship and companionship I've shared with he and his wife, Becky, for as long as I can remember. And thanks are also in order to Mike Vannater for his cover design, and to Larry and Lilliam Larsen for their efforts in turning a manuscript and stack of pictures into the finished product you hold in your hands.

Just as importantly, my appreciation also goes out to you, the hunters, sportsmen, and conservationists all across California and the country. Without you, there wouldn't be any wildlife and wild places left to enjoy.

A Word About Pig Tags and Hog Calling

On July 1, 1992, California began requiring all wild boar hunters to purchase a wild pig tag before hunting hogs in the state. The tags are valid for the hunting license year, which runs July 1 to June 30. Resident hunters may purhase tags at any hunting license agent throughout the state in books of five tags, which cost $7.90. Nonresident pig tags are sold individually, and cost $10 apiece. A valid California hunting license is still required to hunt hogs, in addition to the new tags.

The tag requirement was instituted by the state as a first step in trying to determine exactly how many wild boar hunters there are statewide, as well as how many hogs are harvested by hunters each year. This data will help the state manage the increasing hog population, which will hopefully result in increased hunter opportunity for all California sportsmen.

Have you ever tried calling wild hogs to you? It may sound crazy, but let me asure you that it works. Right after the first edition of this book was written, I began experimenting with calling hogs. Wild boar are gregarious animals, constantly snuffling about, grunting and squealing, and generally staying in touch with other members of its herd vocally. Those experiments resulted in the "Boss Hawg" wild boar call, being made by Haydel's Game Call company.

I've called in and harvested over two dozen wild boar using this call, from dry sows to large, aggressive boars, many with my bow. It's exciting, fun, and a good way to locate hogs that may be bedded up in thick brush, where you'll never see them. Also, if the hogs bust your stalk by either seeing or hearing, but not smelling, you, softly chuckling on a Boss Hawg call with often settle them right down. I've held hogs right in front of me at less than 35 yards this way, even though I was sitting right in the wide open.

Hog calls are hard to find in California sporting goods stores, but there's a convenient order blank in the back of this book to enable you to purchase one, if you so desire. Give it a try on your next hunt. It's great fun!

Bob Robb
March, 1993

4

TABLE OF CONTENTS

CHAPTER 1

INTRODUCTION

What's the number one big game animal in California today, in terms of numbers of animals harvested? Most hunters would say "deer" with little hesitation--and they'd be wrong. In the 1980's, the wild boar overtook deer as the big game animal taken most often by sport hunters, according to estimates compiled by the California Department of Fish and Game.

Even though nearly 300,000 hunters pursue deer in California each year, the total harvest is only around 10 percent, or roughly 30,000 animals. This ranks California dead last among the success rate of all western states. Yet hunters put between 40,000 and 60,000 wild boar in the freezer each year, according to DFG estimates.

I say estimates because, in reality, the DFG has no idea how many hogs are taken by hunters each year. They use hunting license surveys and other questionnaire-type data gatherers for their wild boar information, while deer are monitored by the sale and return of deer tags. The DFG's data banks are also unsure as to the wild boar's exact range throughout the state. In fact, trying to get any definitive information on wild boar from the DFG is like trying to make a proverbial silk purse out of a sow's ear--it can't be done. They really don't have much.

As the popularity of wild boar hunting increases, as it certainly will, the state agency entrusted with the task of nurturing the health and welfare of the resource will hopefully take a bigger interest in what is happening with our wild boar population. Years ago, in a

In terms of the number of animals harvested by hunters each year, wild boar have overtaken deer as California's number one big game animal.

letter to the state Fish and Game Commission, I proposed issuing pig tags to hunters, much like deer tags, at minimal cost and with a mandatory return requirement regardless of whether or not the hunter was successful. In this way the DFG would know exactly how many hunters are out pursuing hogs each year, and specifically where the harvest occurs. Charging hunters a $5 tag fee would stop no one from hunting, and would pay for the cost of issuing and processing these tags, as well as sorting through the ensuing data. Such a program makes sense to me.

Why is wild boar hunting constantly growing in popularity? For one thing, the success rate of hunting on private ranches or with guides who have access to prime private property is virtually 100 percent. Compare that to the 10 percent success rate for deer, and you can see why more and more hunters chase wild hogs every year. On public land, the chances of taking a hog are much less (I'd say no better than 33 percent), but in the better areas it's again a better bet than your chances of tagging a buck.

Season length is another mark in favor of wild boar. In effect,

8

If wild boar hunting is anything at all, it's a fun sport, the ideal way to enjoy the outdoors with your best buddies. It can also easily be combined with hunts for other species with more restricted seasons.

there's no closed season--you can hunt wild hogs all year around. Cost is another plus for wild hog hunting. Private ranch and guided hunts cost much, much less than guided deer hunts throughout the west (see Appendix A for specifics). Of course, public land hunting is free. And with a bag limit of one hog per day, one in possession (two and four in selected places), the opportunity is there to harvest several hogs each year.

The food value of wild boar is another positive. The meat is succulent and lean, as flavorful as any you'll ever have. An average meat pig of 150 to 200 pounds, live weight, will translate into 50 to 75 pounds of boned-out hams, chops, and sausage in the freezer. It's become a staple in my house.

Above and beyond all that, wild boar are just plain fun to hunt. Gregarious in nature, they run together in herds of a few to a bunch, and are interesting to watch as they, well, just act like pigs. They're the ideal animal for a youngster or other novice to hunt, and a private ranch hunt is the perfect family hunting outing. And when other hunting seasons are on, like quail, dove, turkeys and even deer, combining a hunt for wild boar with any of these in many areas is a smart idea.

This book was written in the hope that it will help you enjoy wild boar hunting as much as I do, whether you hunt them guided on private property or with a couple of your buddies on public land. Because of my job I'm fortunate enough to be able to hunt throughout the world each year, and wouldn't trade that for anything. But if the truth be told, I like to hunt wild hogs in California as much as anything I pursue on these other more exotic trips.

Try it once, and you'll be hooked, too.

CHAPTER 2

HOG HISTORY

Long before the sun has poked its nose over the horizon line to warm and brighten another spring day, three hunters have made their way to the crest of a hill. Light sweat shirts are all they need to ward off the chill, a sign that soon even a thin cotton shirt will be too much. Together they sit and whisper, two men and a boy on his first big game hunt ever. All are excited by the day's prospects.

As it gets just light enough to see, the binoculars reveal a small string of wild hogs moving toward their position. Feeding in the grain fields below, the hogs are ready to take their full bellies to the shade and safety of their beds in the thick brush of the hills. The hunters have the wind in their faces, and spread out to get ready.

As the pigs trot closer, the safety catches are softly clicked off. The boy will shoot first, his father pointing out a fat reddish sow at the head of the string. "Easy, son," he cautions softly. "Let her get close, and pick a spot just behind the shoulder." At the proper moment the boy fires, his sow crumpling with the impact of the bullet from his .30-06. In his excitement he never heard the other rifles go off, nor did he see the other two sows drop.

Both men congratulate the boy with smiles, laughter, a shake of the hand and a couple of joking remarks about how, in a year or two, he'll easily be the best shot of the three. They show him how to dress his hog, and he eagerly gets bloody to the elbows in caring for his meat. All three pigs gutted, the largest is placed in the cool shade of an ancient oak, while the larger two are loaded onto pack frames for

11

the two-mile trek to the truck. By lunch time all three are quartered and cooling in ice chests on the way to the neighborhood butcher shop.

Similar scenes are repeated thousands of times each year up and down California as hunters harvest more than twice as many wild boar as they do deer. Yet most of these sportsmen know very little about the history of their quarry, or how the wild boar came to find a home in the foothills of the Golden State.

The European wild boar has been hunted by man for over 40,000 years, according to archaeologists and other scientists. Cave paintings dating back to this early period in man's history show man and large-toothed wild boar in deadly combat. The image of the wild boar found its way into both the art and literature of the ancient Assyrians, Egyptians, Romans, and Greeks. In Greek mythology, the hero Adonis reportedly fell victim to the tusks of a wild boar. There's little doubt that the strong, masculine appearance and aggressive attitude of the wild boar, with his prominent, razor-sharp ivory-like tusks, his oversized testicles, and his ferocious face served to endear the beast to hunters down through the ages.

The wild boar is believed to have had its beginnings in Eurasia and northern Africa, and is the original progenitor of the various modern domestic swine species. (We'll talk more specifically about the boar's physical make-up in Chapter 3, "Boar Biology"). In North America, the wild boar is in reality an immigrant whose ancestors came from the Old World, just as all non-native humans are. The New World's only pig-like animal is the collared peccary, or javelina, an animal that does not belong to the same scientific genus as the wild boar and is, at best, a distant cousin. It is highly likely that both share as an ancestor the gigantic wild hog that roamed portions of the earth during the lower Miocene period, some 25 million years ago.

Domestic swine made their first appearance in the New World in the 16th century with the Spanish explorers. Hernando de Soto is reported to have brought several domestic pigs as part of his animal cargo on a trip to Hispaniola (Cuba) to use as food for his troops and the first settlers. Domestic pigs were subsequently introduced to mainland North America around 1539 into what is now the south-

California's wild boar are a cross between feral pigs brought into the state by the Spanish in the mid-1700's, and pure-strain Russian hogs that came to the state at the beginning of the 20th century. (Photo by Durwood Hollis)

eastern United States. Their succulent meat and the fact that they needed little care from humans to survive and flourish made them very popular, and soon their numbers spread.

In California, the first domestic swine arrived with the Spanish in 1769. The next recorded importation was made by the Russian settlers at their base at Fort Ross, in Sonoma County. At the height of California's gold rush, in the 1850's, settlers hoping to strike it rich brought domestic pigs with them as a cheap, easy-to-care-for food supply. By this time the white men had also brought new strains of disease with them, and these had taken their toll on the state's Indian population. With the California grizzly bear hunted into virtual extinction, the natural competition (Indians and bears) for food was gone, and a new ecological niche opened up. It was soon filled by many of the domestic animals of the settlers. They released their swine to forage on the abundant supply of acorns and wild grains in the foothill country, and the pigs took to this like a duck takes to water.

If wild hogs are anything, they are adaptable, able to live in a wide variety of terrain and climate. This little boar found the perfect hiding spot during a cold winter rain--a small northern California rock cave.

These domestic swine were rarely fenced, and most stayed relatively close to the settlements themselves. However, a few curious individuals wandered off and were never recaptured. The result was a substantial population of wild feral swine running loose in the more inaccessible canyons of the central coast region.

The European wild boar made its way to the new world in a more direct way, being purposely transplanted several different times. Three noteworthy stockings have been recorded. In 1893, a gentleman named Austin Corbin brought 50 animals from the Black Forest of Germany to his private New Hampshire hunting preserve. A small, huntable population of animals can still be found on scattered private properties in this region today. In 1900, 150 to 200 wild boar were again imported from Germany, this time into the Adirondack Mountains of New York state. For whatever reason (probably a combination of a lack of suitable mast foods and an inhospitable climate), this planting did not prove as successful as the one in New Hampshire; all these animals were believed dead by the early 1920's.

The most successful and important transplanting of wild boar

Wild boar continue to expand their range statewide, and now occupy 30 of the state's 50 counties. As their range increases, so do the opportunities to hunt them on both public and private land.

was made by an English gentleman named George Gordon Moore. Moore purchased several wild boar from the Ural Mountains of Russia and, via his agent in Berlin, had them shipped to his 600-acre property at a place called Hooper's Bald in western North Carolina. This took place in 1912, and for eight years no hunting was permitted. In 1920, Moore instituted a controlled European-style of boar hunting, where sportsmen pursued the animals on horseback and dispatched them with long, thick spears. During the course of this hunt several of the boar escaped through the split-rail fence that surrounded the property, and eventually made their way into the rugged Great Smoky Mountains. It didn't take long for the wild boar to meet up with the feral hogs that had been roaming the area since the days of the Spanish conquistadors. The two can freely interbreed, and the result was a wild boar/feral hog cross that remains firmly established in an area that once held only whitetail deer, black bear, and small game.

As an aside, it is interesting to note that these wild hogs have become so firmly entrenched in the Great Smoky Mountains that in

1977 officials of the National Park Service called for their eradication from the Great Smoky Mountains National Park because of the environmental impact their numbers are having. The hogs are eating so much of the natural mast crop (acorns, etc.) that the wild turkeys, deer, and other small game have less to eat in winter. They are also causing damage to the park's streams and other natural waterways with their rooting. However, the residents of Graham County, North Carolina are serious boar hunters, and their subsequent outrage prevented any eradication program. Instead park officials and volunteers began trapping pigs in 1977, releasing them into the nearby Nantahala National Forest, where they may be hunted. The park service learned that even professional hunters couldn't solve the park's pig problems. A similar problem was identified in California's Monterey and Sonoma counties in 1985, where officials also learned the folly of using so-called "professional hunters" to solve their troubles with marauding wild boar.

Moore's work found its way across the continent to California, where three boars and nine sows were released onto the San Francisquito Ranch in Monterey County in the mid-1920's. This was the first documented release of pure-strain wild boar into California. Many people believe that the Russians brought the first wild boar to the state (they brought only domestic pigs), or that publishing magnate William Randolph Hearst released wild boar onto his San Simeon ranch along with other exotic animals (he did not).

Neither the Russians nor Hearst nor the early Spaniards can claim credit for California's wild boar population. Prior to the 1920's, there were small, scattered populations of feral hogs roaming the foothills of the western Sierra Nevada and along various coastal mountain ranges where early settlers had released their domestic swine to roam and forage freely. These domestic-strain pigs, though very adaptable, lacked the genetic make-up to survive harsh changes in weather or minor disease. When the wild boar of the San Francisquito Ranch interbred with these domestic-strain feral hogs (which, knowing the nature of swine both wild and domestic, one can assume they did immediately and frequently), a hardier strain of genetic material was introduced into the population. This allowed the offspring to adapt to and survive in a wider range of weather and

Wild boar hunting occupies a prominent place in the tales of the ancient Greeks, Romans, and other cultures, and is even depicted on cave paintings over 40,000 years old. That legacy continues today up and down California.

disease, and to digest different types of forage. They also became harder to hunt.

Wild boar soon spread through the Santa Lucia Mountains, and were trapped and transplanted up and down the state (including the Channel Islands off the southern California coast, where they can still be found).

Shortly after World War II California's wild boar population began to expand noticeably. Sport hunters were also becoming more and more interested in wild boar, though the state still had a reasonably strong deer population and most big game hunting interest was focused there. By the early 1960's the first full-blown wild boar hunting operations began to spring up, and guided pig hunts became more and more common. By the 1970's, wild boar had gained a foothold in such diverse locations as Santa Barbara County in southern California, the Humboldt County coast in the northwest corner of the state, and the lava beds of Lassen County near the foot of Mount Lassen, near the northern rim of the vast San Joaquin Valley.

Sightings have also been reported near the Oregon border, in Siskiyou County, and along the upper reaches of the Colorado River.

By the early 1980's, wild boar hunting began to supplant deer hunting as the favorite of California's big game hunters. Today the annual wild boar harvest easily exceeds that of deer hunters. Wild boar continue to expand their range, and now are believed to reside in at least 30 of the state's 58 counties.

What does the future hold for wild boar themselves, and the hunters who pursue them in the Golden State? Despite an almost total lack of management by the California Department of Fish & Game, the future is extremely bright.

A call to DFG headquarters in Sacramento reveals that the DFG has virtually no wild boar management plan, nor do they even have any money budgeted to implement one. (According to spokesman Eric Loft, $50,000 was requested for the 1989-90 budget year, but this had not been approved by press time). No population studies have been conducted, and therefore the DFG has no idea just how many wild hogs there are roaming free in the state. The only information they receive on populations is when a depredation permit is requested from a rancher or state or federal park when pigs begin damaging the countryside with their rooting.

There are some groups who want the game mammal status removed from wild boar completely, a move that would make them a varmint rather than a game animal and not subject to DFG-imposed harvest controls. The people making these requests are usually those who fear for the safety of park lands impacted by large hog populations, and would just as soon see every last wild boar in California sent back to Europe.

For several years there has been talk of a $1 wild boar tag being required for all wild boar hunters, to be used much like deer tags. Such a requirement would at least give biologists relatively accurate harvest data, and the fee wouldn't prevent anyone from hunting hogs. To be legal, however, such a fee would require action by the legislature, and such action is not in sight.

In terms of overall annual harvest, for the years 1987 and 1988 (the last years the DFG had any data available at press time),

One of the reasons hogs continue to expand their range is their prolific breeding habits. Once they become established in an area, it is virtually impossible to get rid of them-- they reproduce too fast for that.

estimates are that sport hunters took in the neighborhood of 40,000 wild boar per year, according to the DFG's Loft. These numbers are arrived at by surveying just three percent of hunting license holders, asking them the game the harvested that year, and extrapolating those results to the state's total number of license holders. There are many in the hunting community who question the validity of such surveys, but at the moment they're the best California has.

The general bag and possession limit of one wild boar per day, one in possession, seems to be the way the DFG will go in the near future. However, under the Private Lands Management Program some ranches have been granted a two hog per day limit. The limits on both Santa Cruz and Santa Catalina islands are now two per day, four in possession, for example.

With the absence of any large natural predators and without any natural catastrophe like disease, California's wild boar population can only increase as the years go by. The animals are much more adaptable to human encroachment than are deer, and their prolific breeding habits makes it virtually impossible to hunt, trap, or chase them out of a particular area. Wild boar are without question the state's number one big game animal, both today and in the foreseeable future.

CHAPTER 3

BOAR BIOLOGY

As the sun dipped lower and lower in the western sky, the eyes of young Tommy Lindbergh, a 12-year old hunter from southern California, told a sadder tale than the smile frozen on his lips. Tommy had never been big game hunting before, and his dad, Jack, had thought that a wild boar hunt would be a terrific way to season the boy a bit before taking him to Colorado that October in search of mule deer.

The pigs had vanished that day, as they sometimes do, even though the three of us were hunting a normally very productive private ranch. Both Jack and I had consoled Tommy as best we could, trying to teach him that this was what hunting was all about. Sometimes the game comes easily, sometimes tough, and sometimes it just doesn't come at all. We'd had a good day together, swapping stories and enjoying the wild flowers, the quail and other small game, the hawks soaring on the midday thermals, the deer we'd jumped from their beds along a protected canyon rim.

When the first hogs finally showed themselves an hour or so before dark, Tommy didn't believe me at first when I told him to get ready. He had seen the string of 10 animals, too, but thought they were dogs or cows--anything but wild boar. We got close, and Tommy dropped a fat meat sow with a single shot from an old Remington Model 721 in .30-06. His dad had shortened the stock to fit the youngster, and Tommy shot it well, the 180-grain bullet taking the pig right behind the front shoulder at 75 yards.

21

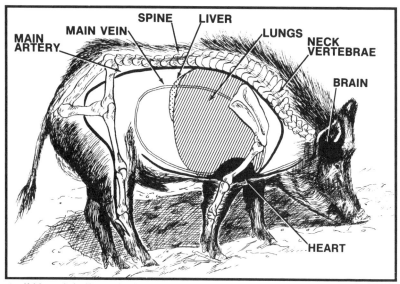

A wild boar is built much like its close cousin, the black bear, built low to the ground with big bones, powerful front shoulders, and small hips. The heart is located low and forward in the chest. (Photo courtesy Petersen's HUNTING magazine)

This scene is vivid in my mind, even though it happened almost 20 years ago. I've guided lots of other hog hunters since, and been in on hundreds of other boar kills, but I remember Tommy's ear-to-ear grin almost as much as his wondering just whatinheck those animals really were when he first saw them.

Literally thousands and thousands of hunters pursue wild boar in California each year without knowing a thing about the animals. They just assume that they're nothing more than wild pigs, and leave it at that. To me, learning as much as I can about the animals I hunt is a big part of the enjoyment of the total experience. And it's true that the more you know about your quarry, the better your chances of finding them on a regular basis.

As we learned in Chapter 2, wild boar are the original progenitors of all the world's domestic swine. It is unclear where the first wild boar were found on earth, but it is pretty well agreed that the first were residents of northern Africa and Eurasia.

In California, the wild pigs we are hunting today are a cross

The broad, blunt hooves of a wild hog are quite different from the narrow, pointed hooves of deer. They help the animal get excellent traction in soft, muddy soil. (Photo by Durwood Hollis)

between the pure-strain European wild boar first introduced into the state in the early 20th century, and the feral swine they met in the foothills of the central coast. When you see a wild boar in the field today, you can't be absolutely sure just how much of the "wild" strain it actually carries at first glance. Both pure-strain European wild boar and domestic pigs are members of the scientific genus *Sus Scrofa* and can freely interbreed. The difference is in the chromosome count. A pure-strain wild boar will have a total of 36 chromosomes, while a pure domestic hog will have 38 chromosomes. When two pure-strain animals mate, the resulting piglets possess 37 chromosomes. However, let the offspring interbreed, and you now have a litter of piglets that may have 36, 37, or 38 chromosomes, whatever happens to please that particular molecule of DNA at the moment.

The vast disparity in appearance of each individual wild boar you find in the world today is the result of this chromosomal difference. Hunt the hogs a while, and soon you'll see these individual differences that may seem subtle at first glance, but really tell you a lot.

Some hogs just "look" wilder than others, and the reason is simple-- they have fewer chromosomes than some.

And a wild appearance is important to most hunters, who desire hogs that as closely resemble the pure-strain European boar as they can find. The look is distinctive.

In years past, there were a few unscrupulous hunting "guides" who bought domestic hogs at auction, placed them in pens, booked clients and, unbeknownst to the hunters, released the penned hogs just before the hunting party came around the corner. These unwitting sportsmen were soon bragging about their 800-pound trophy hogs, and even had their photographs published in weekly outdoor newspapers. These pale-colored pigs had floppy ears on a dish-shaped face and curly tails, and were no more "wild" than the local preacher. Wild hogs look nothing like this.

The wild hogs roaming the hills of California look the part. They have a laterally-compressed body profile, a straight tail that hangs down between the hind legs (except when it's switching away bothersome flies in hot weather), slim hips and large front shoulders, relatively long legs, and a long, pointy snout. Compared to the domestic lard pig, it has a dense covering of long body hair, with a mane or "comb" of long erect bristles along the neck and spine.

As is the case with all wild creatures, Mother Nature gave the wild boar these characteristics for a reason. The large front shoulders are extremely powerful, and serve to pull the boar up and around the hilly country he has always called home. They also help him get leverage when rooting for food. Beneath those overly-large shoulders is an equally large chest cavity that houses a good-sized heart and pair of lungs. A wild boar has an excellent aerobic capacity, and can both sprint extremely quickly straight ahead like a fullback and fall into a ground-eating trot that would make a distance runner envious. With his long, strong legs carrying him easily over uneven terrain, I have pushed a 300-pound-class boar over a plowed field in a pick-up truck doing 25 miles an hour for three miles before the hog lost me in a brushy canyon. A chase like that will open your eyes to how much ground a big hog can cover when he's of a mind. The feet are narrow and have four hoofed toes; the side toes, or dewclaws, don't touch the ground when the animal walks, but may leave tracks

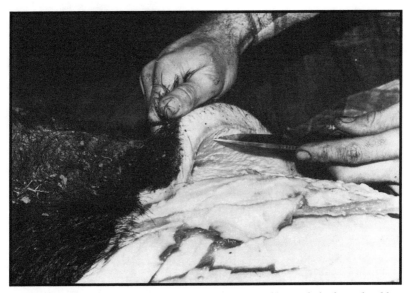

The thick cartilaginous sheath, or "armor plating," found beneath the front shoulders of a big boar can be well over one inch thick. It helps protect the animal from the tusks of other boars during combat.

in soft soil. The wild boar is the only split-hoofed animal of the Pacific states that has a single stomach and doesn't chew its cud.

The long, slender snout enables a boar to root up the ground, the practice used to search for food. Wild boar will turn over logs, cow patties, and rocks in search of insects, grubs, earthworms, roots, berries--you name it. They'll even eat lizards, small rodents, and like the larvae of crane flies, often found near oak trees. Like man, they are very omnivorous, meaning they will eat meat and plants both, and wild boar are truly the "junk food junkies" of California's big game animals. They will literally eat anything when preferred foods-- acorns and harvestable grain crops like barley and wheat--aren't plentiful. I've seen them eat each other; big boars are well known for eating the tender young of a newborn litter of their own kind. One of the largest boars I've ever shot was taken right off the carcass of a dead cow, and I once saw a big sow and litter of 10 piglets right up inside a dead cow's carcass, eating it from the inside out.

Their eyes are set far back in the head to protect them from

A wild hog has an excellent aerobic capacity, enabling it to cover distances of three or four miles at a speed of over 20 miles an hour. The animal is also extremely quick in close quarters.

sharp objects while rooting, though the animals are so blind you wonder why nature even bothered with that detail. Unlike the floppy ears of the barnyard hog, a wild boar's ears are erect.

The bristly coat of hair is thin in summer, and thicker in cooler climates. In the coldest portions of the animal's range in northern California, where snows sometimes fall, they will even grow a thick undercoat of curly wool just like their brethren in the forests and mountains of Europe and Asia. The coat can be a multitude of colors, ranging from a dark grayish-black to reddish brown. Those hogs with more of a wild strain in them will be a solid color in this range, with the grayish hairs thicker over the belly and jowls in a gristled pattern not unlike that of the grizzly bear. This shouldn't be all that surprising, since wild boar are close cousins of the bears.

Those hogs with unsolid coloration probably have more of a feral ancestry to them, and they can be interesting. I've seen just about every pattern under the sun, from black-and-white spotted hogs to belted hogs (a dark body with a light-colored "belt" running down the shoulder) to one 250-pound sow I shot once with a muzzle-loader that was half-and-half--black from the front shoulders forward, and white the rest of the way back.

Males have more of a muscular appearance than sows, as is the case with most species of big game in North America. They aren't necessarily larger on the scales, however. The average wild boar will stand 30 inches high at the shoulder and measure four to five feet in length. Adults can weigh up to 600 pounds on the hoof, but that's extremely unusual. A large male will weigh 300 pounds, and a good-sized female 200 pounds.

Under the massive shoulders of a big boar is the "armor plate" many hunters have heard about. This plate is really a sheath of keratin, or cartilage, placed their to protect the animal when he fights with his own kind. (Two boars fighting is something to see, a battle to the death where neither combatant will give any quarter). This sheath can be over one-inch thick, and can cause problems for hunters, as we'll see later. Skin any old boar, and you'll find numerous scars in this sheath from old fights. One 350-pound boar I shot a few years back had several old scars in the shoulder area that were filled with a foul-smelling pus-like paste as the animal fought off infection. It didn't taint the flavor of the sausage one bit. If you slap your hand against the side of a large boar you've just killed, it will produce a hollow sound almost like slapping the side of a ripe watermelon.

Only males have the large tusks wild boar are so famous for, though sows have smaller, less distinct tusks of their own. There are two uppers and two lowers, with the tusks continuously filed down by working against each other. This constant filing action keeps even the oldest, largest boars from having lower tusks of over three inches in length, though some freaks have grown them as large as 11 inches. The filing action also keeps the edges very sharp, and more than one careless hunter has needed stitches after an encounter with the business end of these teeth.

Tusk length is a poor indicator of a boar's age or size. In the larger-bodied boars the tusks are often broken off from fighting or other accidents. Barrow hogs, those boars captured in traps when young and castrated, often have small bodies and long tusks. And the lower tusks are not always the longest. I saw a strange hog once on the Dye Creek Preserve in northern California that had his lowers broken off--and upper tusks that were at least four inches long. The uppers rarely exceed two inches, and are usually half that size.

There are three reasons why wild boars are increasing their range throughout the state at the fast rate they are. First, while a growing population of coyotes, bobcats, and mountain lions take their share of piglets, there are no other significant predators except man. Second, their omnivorous nature means there's lots to eat, especially on and near grain-growing ranches. And third, they are very prolific breeders.

After giving birth to a litter, sows will usually spend the day in a sheltered bedding area. The litter can number anywhere between three and 12, with the piglets weighing less than a pound at birth after a gestation period of 112 to 115 days. The piglets suckle for approximately 12 weeks, with the boars taking no part in the raising of the young. By nine months of age the young pigs will weigh nearly 100 pounds. They become sexually mature at 18 months, and grow to full size by five or six years. Under ideal circumstances, they have been known to live as long as 27 years.

Once the piglets cease suckling and need little else in the way of physical care from their mother, she will come into heat again. A sow will have two to three litters a year, with approximately half the young surviving to maturity. With those kinds of numbers, it's easy to see how the pig population in a given area can explode seemingly overnight.

Many people believe that wild hogs are dirty animals, but this old wife's tale has little basis in fact. In reality they are one of the cleanest animals in California, wallowing in mud only to cool themselves or get rid of fleas, ticks, and other bothersome pests. The sows and young--and it's common to see a sow in the company of young of two different age classes--usually travel together. The older boars like to live alone or in small bachelor groups, joining the sows only when one comes into heat. As we've seen, that can literally be anytime.

Wild hogs have sensory abilities similar to their close cousins, the black bear. Their hearing is acute, though they sometimes can't hear approaching danger over the noises they themselves make. They are

A barrow hog, like this 150-pounder I shot at Dye Creek, will often be small in the body but carry long tusks. They also make excellent eating pigs. Dye Creek manager Chuck Harrison helps me show it off.

almost blind, able to visually detect only vague shapes and no color. They are very good at detecting movement, however. Their number one defense mechanism is the sense of smell. I believe that wild hogs have as good or better noses than any big game animal in North America. They can smell human odor more than a mile off, if the wind is right, and will usually bolt at the first faint whiff. They can locate food buried a foot underground and even a few inches underwater using only the sense of smell.

Wild boar are almost a nocturnal animal, being most active after dark, in the early morning, and just after dusk. The exception is on a cool, overcast day, when they might be seen moving at any time. During midday they hole up in their beds, which are often found in the thickest brush on hills and mountainsides, or in deep canyons. They will often bed at the base of a large tree, and seem to like using oaks for this purpose. In the canyons and on steep hillsides, the pigs will root out large beds able to hold entire family groups. They'll also bed in small caves, depressions, and other areas that offer protection from the heat of midday, and from predators.

In hot weather hogs must water daily, and often will water twice a day if not bothered. After feeding during the night, they will move to a water hole, where they'll drink their fill and often wallow in the cool mud for a bit before heading off to bed for the day. On the evening trek back to the feeding area they'll again stop to water and wallow.

Any water source is fine with a wild hog. I've seen them drink and wallow in tiny depressions that were almost solid mud, in larger ponds, and have even seen them climb right up into a metal stock tank built for cattle. One hot July day I saw three sets of ears, eyes and snouts peeking over the rim of a full-to-the-brim stock tank on a central coast ranch; the pigs were acting as though it were their own private swimming pool. I half expected them to ask me for a glass of iced tea on my way by.

The more time you spend around wild boar, the more they will fascinate you. They are interesting animals with a storied past tied closely to the history of man. And as is the case with all game, the more a sportsman learns about them, the more successful he will be-- and the more that success will mean to him as well.

CHAPTER 4

MEAT PIG OR TROPHY BOAR?

Wild boar hunters generally fall into two categories--the meat hunter and the trophy hunter. It is very important that you define exactly which one you are before heading afield. Are you interested in stuffing the freezer with some of the best-tasting meat around? Or, are you more concerned with looking for a big old boar that will make a terrific-looking mount for the den wall? Your hunting style and, if you're hunting with a guide or on a private ranch, your wallet, will both be affected by your decision.

A meat hog is easy to define. When we're afield, we generally consider any sow, from a young adult to a big, strapping animal, as a good meat pig. The young adult may weigh as little as 80 or 90 pounds on the hoof, or as much as 250 to 350 pounds, live weight. Anything falling within these ranges will generally provide the best eating in the world of wild hogs.

Many people feel that boars never make good eating pigs, but this simply is not true. Young boars are excellent on the table, especially those weighing between 100 and 200 pounds live weight. Barrow hogs--boars that have been trapped and castrated in their youth--are perhaps the best of all meat hogs. Barrow boars forget all about the breeding urge, and therefore don't spend their lives fighting and running around like a teenage boy at puberty. Instead they spend their days eating, relaxing, and putting on weight, and their meat in tender and full of flavor. Without fighting, they don't run the risk of breaking their tusks in combat, either. I've seen

A true trophy boar in anyone's book, this 275-pounder had 3 1/4-inch lower tusks, classically-shaped ears and nose, and dark black coloration. I found him feeding on the carcass of a dead cow.

several barrow boars that wouldn't weigh 150 pounds sporting tusks well over two-inches in length.

Some first-time hunters refuse to take a shot at an excellent meat hog because the color of its coat is not the color they want. These folks forget that you don't eat the hide. Coat color has absolutely nothing to do with the quality of a meat hog. It could be lime green with purple spots for all I care. If it's the size and sex I want, I'll take it for the pot.

I actually get a kick out of taking the ugliest hogs I can find for meat pigs. It's gotten to be sort of a running joke with my friends. There can be a herd of beautiful-looking all-black sows and young boars all in a neat little row, and I'll shoot the spotted sow with one ear ripped off for my meat pig. My hunting buddies and me will even have a contest of sorts, seeing who can shoot the sorriest-looking meat hog on a given hunt. It's great fun, and in no way diminishes the flavor of the smoked chops and hams.

The best eating pigs, in my opinion, are pregnant sows that weigh

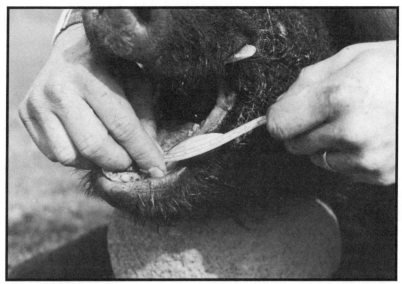

Most guides and hunters consider any boar with lower tusks measuring over two-inches in length to be of trophy caliber. A hog with 2 3/4-inch-or-better tusks is a real monster.

around 150 pounds on the hoof. These lactacting pigs are tender, in prime condition, and have a bit more fat than sows that have just weaned a litter. Young boars in the 100- to 150-pound range also have tender, succulent meat, and are prime candidates for freezer pigs. If I have a choice from a herd of hogs, I'll always take a young sow as my meat pig.

One note on meat sows. Before taking a sow, make sure she isn't nursing a litter of young. With a lone sow and litter, that's easy to determine. In a herd situation, it may take a few minutes to sort things out. Look for an extended belly or protruding teats to help identify a nursing sow. Once a mother is removed, the young are left to fend for themselves. They have little chance for survival in a world where everything--coyotes, bobcats, mountain lions, even old boars-- eat little pigs.

Trophy-class boars are a different story. A trophy hog is defined by most hunters, ranch owners, and guides as any boar having lower teeth (tusks) that measure more than two-inches in length from the gum line. In the real world of pig hunting, finding a boar that meets

33

The best meat pigs of all are pregnant sows weighing between 100 and 150 pounds on the hoof. The protruding belly and teats are the giveaway. I photographed this 100-pounder on public land after I had already taken my freezer hog.

this minimum isn't really all that difficult, especially if you are hunting one of the state's better private ranches. Finding a hog with teeth measuring better than 2 1/2-inches is much more difficult. And finding a boar that has three-inch or better tusks--the 28-inch mule deer of hog hunting--is difficult indeed. If you manage to take one of these monsters, buy yourself a Lotto ticket on the way home; your luck just may stay red-hot. There just aren't that many of them around.

While most guides and ranch owners judge a trophy boar by .tusk length alone, the discriminating hunter looks at other criteria, too. Most of us will never have more than one wild boar mounted, so it pays to find one that's exactly what you want before taking him to the taxidermist.

I like to look at a boar's facial characteristics as well as his tusk length. Does he have a pointed snout, indicating lots of true wild Russian genes? Are the ears sharply pointed, not round and floppy? Is the end of the nose flat? Do the teeth--both uppers and lowers--

Judging the body size of hogs can be deceptive, especially when the same size is running together. The height of this barley--12 inches--tells you these hogs probably weigh only 80 pounds each, too small to shoot.

push the lip up prominently? In terms of facial characteristics, I also like a boar who has a rip or two in his ears, showing that he is a fighter. I've seen a couple of old bruisers who had faces that looked like they had been whipped with a weed whacker. I like that in a boar.

I also judge a trophy boar by the color of his coat. Most true trophy hunters want a hog that is pure black, and they do make impressive mounts. A really interesting color is a coal-black coat with silvery-gray guard hairs. True Russian hogs have a twinge of red in their hair. If you spend lots of time hunting hogs, you'll see boars with trophy-length tusks in all color phases under the sun, from deep black to red to black-and-white to spotted to checkerboarded to multi-colored (like a calico cat) to pure white. You have to decide if tusk length is more important to you than color.

Personally, I'm still looking for the perfect hog to mount. I saw him once, on a central coast ranch, and never got a shot at him. He was deep auburn all over, with a row of razorback hair that ran the length of the backbone all the way up to the back of his head. He had

Sacramento Bee outdoor editor *Gary Voet is happy as can be with this 140-pound sow, a hog that will translate into about 50 pounds of cut-and-wrapped meat for his freezer. Guide Mike Ballew helped Gary find her.*

the classic Russian facial characteristics, and polished tusks that really stood out. He was moving quickly through the brush and a shot would have been chancy, so I held off and hoped he'd pop out into an adjacent field. I never saw him again but if and when I do, I'll take him even if I'm really hunting for a meat pig.

That point illustrates the overriding factor in trophy hunting: a trophy is a trophy in the eye of the beholder. You may want to mount a certain hog because he looks great to you, not someone else, and that's the way it should be. I once shot a big old boar on the Camp 5 ranch that was very tempting. He was big in the body, weighing an honest 320 pounds live weight on the ranch scales. He was deep gray all over and caked with mud. He had ripped-up ears, a scarred face, and deep tusk wounds on both shoulders that had healed with time. His tusks were short, though, broken off through constant fighting and measuring under two-inches in length on both sides. Nonetheless, he was a true trophy boar in every sense of the word, an old battler who had fathered countless offspring and ruled his world for years. He just wasn't the kind of hog I wanted for my wall, though he may have been exactly what another hunter would want.

I finally shot a mounting pig on the Dye Creek ranch in the winter of 1988. He's the big boar on the back cover of this book, a Russian-looking dark-colored fighter with 3 1/4-inch tusks that weighed nearly 275 pounds on the hoof. To me he's the classic representative of a California wild boar, a hog I've waited a long time to get. I'm awfully proud to have him.

With these old boars, the meat can be a bit on the tough side and a little gamey tasting, although if the hogs have been feeding on barley and other cereal grains the flavor tends to mellow. Instead of having pigs this size butchered in a regular manner, I have the hams smoked and the rest turned into a spicy ground sausage or one-pound salami sticks. It's very edible this way, but as we said at the beginning of this chapter, if you're looking for the ultimate meat pig, these are not the kinds of hogs to be shooting.

Evaluating Tusk Length

The toughest part of judging a trophy boar in the field is trying to evaluate the tusk length. There are so many variables involved that even guides who have looked over literally thousands of hogs over the years can get fooled. There are a couple of rules of thumb to go by, but in all honesty I've been tricked so often that I'm a bit skeptical of them. I go by instinct and feel now, and I still get it wrong. That's easy to do when the difference between a good trophy and a superb one is no more than a quarter-inch of tooth.

The big problem in trophy tusk evaluation lies in the fact that the tusk is mostly hidden from view by the lips. That's why many guides carry a spotting scope with them. They like to get a big boar in the open and really zoom in on those lower teeth. If you have that kind of time it helps immeasurably, but unfortunately the hogs don't always cooperate.

You also must be sure to look at <u>both</u> lower teeth. I can't tell you the number of times I've seen a hunter get all excited and shoot his trophy boar because one tusk looked great. Then when they got to the downed hog and rolled him over, they found that the other tusk had been broken at least in half. A true trophy boar has good tusk length on both sides.

The basic rule of thumb says that if you can see at least one inch of lower-tusk ivory clearly exposed, the boar will go over two-inches, and there's a good chance he will go more than that. The variables involved? The tusks could be muddy or stained, and be longer or shorter than they appear through the binoculars. The lips can be puffed, not showing enough tooth, or they can be thin, giving the illusion that there's more than meets the eye. Some boars have large heads, some have small heads. The light might be bad, casting shadows on the tusks. You might have dust in your eye, stayed up too late the night before and have blurry vision, or be worried about a business problem and not concentrating enough.

You get the picture. The variables involved are great. That's where it pays to have an experienced guide along to help you judge, and give you an expert opinion before you shoot. Just keep in mind that no one can make the decision to shoot except you. If you have doubts, if the boar isn't exactly what you want, pass on him and keep looking. It's your pig and nobody else's. Don't be pressured into shooting if you aren't 100 percent sure that's what you want to do. And remember that even if you are sure beyond a shadow of a doubt that he's the one you want, you may be disappointed in the tusk length once you get over to him.

Some hunters look at that as a real tragedy. I look at it as a good excuse to come hunting again.

CHAPTER 5

HOW TO HUNT HOGS

Big game hunting throughout the West--and much of the world, for that matter--is not the mysterious, difficult task that many people believe it to be. To read the various sporting magazines and watch the latest how-to videos, you'd think that you have to be part Olympic athlete and part magician to consistently take good heads of game. The truth of the matter is that any average person, in relatively good physical condition who shoots his weapon competently, can do well time after time.

That's not to say that big game animals are going to let you carelessly waltz in and tack their hide to the wall, because they're not. As in any endeavor in life, whether it be business or pleasure, the person who studies the game, puts in the extra effort, and isn't afraid to get out there and make a few mistakes through personal experience, is the one who will succeed consistently. They say that it's better to be lucky than good, but I'm a firm believer that you can make your own luck more often than not. In my travels around the world, I've found that the formula for success goes something like this: hard work + field experience + knowledge of the terrain + an understanding of the quarry's habits = good luck, and success.

In hog hunting, taking a pig can be easy or it can be hard. There are days when you can do everything right, even on the best private ranches, and the animals just aren't going to cooperate. In Chapters 6 and 7 we'll discuss the difficulties of hunting public land today, and in Chapter's 8 and 9 we'll talk about hunting private lands, where the

Wild hogs are most active right at sunrise and sundown, especially during hot weather. Do whatever it takes to be in position to glass for them well before it begins to get light.

living--and the hunting--is relatively easy. But no matter where you go pig hunting in the Golden State, keep in mind that there will be days when you will not get a shot. It's those days when you need to remember that you're in the field to enjoy the great outdoors, revel in the wonders of Mother Nature, be as one with the wild and at peace with yourself. Hunting is much more than killing, it's also a mind set that allows us to experience nature at the basest level. If you're in the field just to "kill something," you're missing the point, and will never understand the true joys of the hunt.

Know the Game, Know the Terrain

Before discussing specific hunting methods for hogs, you need to understand the basic formula for success. That formula is "know the game, know the terrain." If you first understand the basic needs and habits of pigs, you'll know how they will react to changes in their environment. Then, if you also know the terrain you'll be hunting, you'll have a very good idea of where the pigs will be given certain

Hog droppings are large and round, especially when they are feeding on grain or mast crops; they look nothing like deer droppings. A .30-06 cartridge gives perspective as to their size.

environmental parameters (weather, feed and water conditions, time of day, hunting pressure, etc.).

In Chapter 3 we talked about the biological needs of wild hogs, as well as their basic habits. Pigs will alter their habits if they're pressured heavily by hunters, but not that much. It takes lots of pressure to move them off their preferred schedule, if there is plenty of food, water, and cover nearby. Find hogs in a certain place today, and the chances are good that you can find them there tomorrow, or the next day, or the next week, if the basic environmental conditions have not changed.

Knowing the terrain cannot be overemphasized. One of the big advantages of hunting private property is that the ranch owner or guide knows his property like you know your own back yard, and he can predict where the pigs will be on a given day, at a given time. When hunting public land, using topographical maps will give you a good idea of what to expect, but not until you've paid your dues and walked the ground several times will you become familiar with the terrain. This hands-on experience is invaluable. Those hunters willing to pay the price in time and sweat to learn public hunting areas can do well. Those who are not willing to do so will find themselves literally wandering around in the dark; their chances for success are hit or miss. This will be discussed in detail in Chapter 6.

Before going any further, let's quickly review the strengths and weaknesses of a wild hog's defenses. As discussed in Chapter 3, wild pigs have tremendous noses. The sense of smell is their first line of defense. With that in mind, wind direction and thermal currents should be your number one consideration when hunting these animals. They can smell you a long, long way away if you're upwind of them, and all it takes is one whiff of human odor and they're long gone. Their sense of hearing is good, but not great. Keep from talking, slamming car doors, rattling metal together, etc., and you'll be ok. When stalking, don't kick any rocks or snap any twigs, either. The most vulnerable sense a wild hog has is its eyesight. Pigs really are next to blind, and this is to your advantage. However, they're not totally blind. They can see movement, and if you come strolling in when they're looking right at you they'll spook for sure. However, you can be sitting right in the open and have hogs walk right up to you, if you remain quiet and still and the wind is right.

Wild hogs also possess excellent speed and stamina. Once spooked, they can run for miles, both uphill and downhill. I've clocked them in a pickup truck on a private ranch at 25 miles an hour over broken ground, a speed one old boar kept up for nearly three miles before he ran out of gas and ducked into some heavy brush, mouth agape and panting. Just because they look a little awkward with those big front shoulders and tiny hips, don't be deceived and underestimate their speed. It's impressive.

Basic Hunting Methods

There are four basic methods used to hunt wild hogs. These are take-a-stand, spot-and-stalk, driving, and the use of hounds. Let's see how to use each to our advantage.

On a typical wild boar hunt, the first thing you'll do in the morning is <u>take a stand</u>. You know there are pigs using the area,

Rub trees--where hogs scratch their backs--indicate the presence of pigs as well as their size. Rub trees are found near water, and are often caked with mud and hair.

feeding on nearby grain or acorns or whatever, and you've selected a vantage point that gives a commanding view of the area. Ideally you've got a little cover and a good rest to shoot from. The stand also offers you some flexibility, in that if the hogs aren't exactly where you thought they'd be you can move and intercept them.

When taking a stand first thing in the morning, the key is to be in position a good hour before daylight. Often hogs are moving to bedding areas before sun-up, and if you're hunting feed areas you need to be open for business the minute it's light enough to shoot. A half-hour after the first glow of daybreak illuminates the eastern sky may be too late, the best hunting of the day wasted. Also, by getting to your stand this early you allow the world to return to a natural state before shooting time. This gives any animals in the area a chance to settle down and act naturally, forgetting about the intruder--you--that's entered their domain. This is especially true during periods of hot weather, when hogs like to be bedded as early in the morning as possible.

Stands aren't just used on feed areas, however. If you're hunting away from a grain field, for example, a good spot to place a stand is on a travel route between feed and bedding areas. You can often catch hogs as they move to their daytime sleeping areas. These types of stands can be very productive if you're hunting public lands that border private ranches that won't give you permission to hunt.

Water holes are another excellent stand spot, especially in summer. Wild hogs water every day, and when the weather's hot they'll often climb right into the water hole to cool down, or wallow in the mud. I can vividly remember seeing three small boars grunt and groan their way right up into a metal stock tank on a hot summer's day as I sat in a tree stand not 15 yards away with my bow. They played around for an hour or so, enjoying the cool respite from the 90 degree day, until one stretched out over the edge of the tank to climb down and my arrow found his lungs. Water holes are very good places for an archery hunter to take a stand, as he can premeasure ranges to help him place his arrow perfectly.

The key to choosing a stand sight is wind direction. In good pig areas it pays to have a couple of different stand sites selected, choosing the one you'll hunt on any given morning with the wind direction in mind. Wind direction is more important than cover.

You can always bring along a little camouflage netting for cover, but there isn't a thing you can do about the wind. You also need to have open shooting lanes that permit you to point and fire your weapon with a minimum of movement and no worry about tree branches, rocks, brush, or other obstacles that might hinder the shot.

The advantages of taking a stand are many. Being on stand before daylight lets you see everything that's happening in the area without the game seeing you. And, if the animals are moving and you've selected a good stand sight, you let them come to you, not the other way around. Letting the quarry do the moving forces them to make the mistake of showing themselves. If you're hidden on stand and the wind's right, they won't know you're even in the neighborhood. Neither will other animals with better vision and hearing-- deer and wild turkeys, for example--that are much easier to spook, and can in turn cause the hogs to spook and run.

If you don't see any hogs from the early-morning stand, or if you see pigs but they won't be moving in your direction, it's time to employ the <u>spot and stalk</u> method. Simply stated, spot-and-stalk

In cattle country, hogs love to root among cow plops, picking kernels of undigested grain from them. The freshness will tell you if there are hogs in the vicinity.

hunting means that you move along, looking for game (usually with binoculars), locating hogs, then preparing to stalk in close enough for a shot. It's the primary method most of us use to hunt deer here in the West.

It's a simple concept, but not always that simple to execute. A sudden change in the wind can ruin your stalk. You might stumble across game you didn't see before that spooks, and it in turn sends the hogs running for cover. You may spot pigs on a distant hillside and have to go out of sight of them to make your stalk, only to find them ungraciously gone when you finally reach the spot. There are a million and one things that could go wrong when hunting this way, but it has definite advantages.

For one thing, you cover lots of country this way. For another, it's a method that can be successful even during the heat of midday, when hogs are bedded in thick brush. You just pussyfoot along in bedding areas, glassing up into the brush until you locate sleeping pigs. Of course, this can take lots of time and patience, but it sure produces. You might also elect to move along until you come to thick

Hogs cross under fences, often leaving hair in the wire. Soft, pliable hair is fresh; setting up a stand on this trail would be a good idea. Dry, brittle hair is old; who knows when the hogs passed through here?

brush patches and try to drive the pigs out, a method we'll talk about in a moment.

Proper clothing is essential to successful stalking. You need to be comfortable, and not wear nylon outerwear that will make raspy, screeching sounds as it passes through brush. Cotton and woolen outerwear is preferred for its quiet. New "high-tech" clothing featuring fleece is also excellent for sneaking around the woods during cool weather, while garments of soft, quiet Supplex nylon are outstanding in hot temperatures. Boots should not be heavily Vibram-soled. Instead choose boots with softer, quieter soles. Some of my friends stalk in running-type shoes. Quality binoculars are critical as well. I prefer 10X glasses, but 7X and 8X are fine. Specific hunting gear will be discussed more thoroughly in Chapter 13.

Most hunters blow the stalk at the end, not the beginning. Impatience is their worst enemy, a lack of patience that gets them too nervous in heavy cover to take the time necessary to get an open shot. When hog hunting, the stalking hunter has all the advantages, if the wind's right. There's no reason not to get a high-percentage

Bedding areas are good places to find midday pigs. Beds are made by rooting the earth with the snout, and deepened by constant use. Look for beds on brushy hillsides in shaded areas near food and water sources.

shot, if you take your time. Move slowly and carefully, taking care not to make any unnecessary noises or sudden movements that might alert the hogs. Keep the wind right, and if possible the sun at your back or at least quartering off your shoulders to reduce glare. Remember, there's no hurry. You've got all the time in the world, and besides, isn't that why you came hunting in the first place?

I probably employ the spot-and-stalk method in 90 percent of all my hunting today, and hunting wild boar is no exception. To me, it's the most fun, the most challenging, and the most rewarding.

During midday hours, when hogs are in their beds, is the time to consider a <u>drive</u>. Drives can be very productive, but they can also be hit-and-miss. Even if there are a scad of hogs in the brush patch you're driving, it may be thick enough that you'll never see the hog you want a shot at. You may also only see glimpses of pigs as they race through the thicket, again presenting no decent shot. And if there is more than one shooter stationed near a thicket, the pigs have been known to stay between the hunters, not giving anyone a safe shot (how they do this is one of the great mysteries of the universe, but

If you're hunting big boars but haven't seen any, one indicator that they are in the area is a small-diameter tree that's been chewed on. Boars regularly sharpen their tusks on these little trees.

believe me when I tell you it happens all the time).

There are several ways to drive hogs that have holed up in heavy brush. The most obvious is to position a shooter or shooters south of the brush patch, and send other hunters in the north side. If the brush piles are located in the bottom or along the sides of a ditch or canyon, place hunters on both sides before sending the drivers through. Make sure the drivers move slowly and make lots of racket.

Another way to move hogs is to place a hunter on each side of a brushy canyon. Move slowly along the edge in tandem, throwing rocks and sticks into the brush. Often you'll see the pigs your partner has moved, and vice versa.

I've had some success on windy days by placing shooters down-wind of a brush pile, then sending another person upwind of the cover. He should move near the brush slowly, with a minimum of

There are several ways to hunt hogs, all of which are effective at times. Pick the method best suited to the terrain and conditions, and you'll be feasting on a succulent ham come Sunday dinner time.

noise, and let his scent drift into the cover. The combination of scent and quiet makes the pigs nervous, and they'll often come bolting out like they've been shot from a cannon when noisemaking sends them out cautiously. After a bit, if no hogs come out, the driver may toss a small rock or two, or deliberately snap a dry stick, to try and startle the hogs into action. You just have to play it by ear, keeping in mind that the only correct thing to do is whatever gets the pigs up and moving.

Position shooters intelligently. Look for game trails and other openings that will offer clear shots should the pigs come that way, and be in position to take advantage of them. Don't assume that you'll have forever and a day to get a shot off, either. Driven pigs will be moving out at least at a fast walk, and you'll have to shoot relatively quickly as they wind their way through the brush. Just make sure that you do take enough time to place the shot carefully.

Hunting with hounds is the fourth method you can use. Hound hunting is legal in California, though relatively few practice it when compared to other hunting methods. When hound hunting, the dog handler turns the hounds loose in a good pig area, and they locate pigs by scent. Then the chase is on, and it can be something! Hounds barking and baying, dust flying, pigs snapping their teeth, all usually happening in thick brush with limited visibility.

I've only taken a couple of pigs with dogs. One was shot at a range of half a foot when he turned in the chest-high manzanita and decided he'd had enough of this foolishness. It was certainly exciting, and I'm not sure what would have happened had I not gotten the rifle barrel in position quickly.

Some guides that favor the use of hounds use dogs that they also run bears and cats with, and these dogs are usually excellent pig catchers. Others have packs of hounds they use for hogs and nothing else. A cornered wild boar, with his upper body strength, quickness, and razor-sharp tusks, can take a toll on inexperienced hounds, so it's important that the guide you go hound hunting with has at least a couple of experienced pig dogs in his pack.

In some country, the terrain makes the use of dogs the only sensible way to harvest hogs. If you have the chance to hunt wild boar with hounds, don't pass it up. More often than not, it's an exciting experience, and very successful.

CHAPTER 6

HUNTING ON PUBLIC LAND

Though the day wasn't hot any longer, I wasn't sweating any less. For three hours now my hunting partner and I had been struggling with pack frames loaded down with nearly 90 pounds of fresh wild boar, yet we were still a mile of straight-up from the truck.

The fun had long gone out of this adventure. We had slept on the ground the night before, ignoring the mosquitoes and dust as best we could. The alarm had sounded like a bomb exploding in my ear at 4:00 a.m., but by 4:30 a.m. the excitement of the hunt had overtaken us and we were on our way into a small block of Bureau of Land Management-administered public land in the central coast region. Two hours later we were overlooking small pockets of open country in among the thickly brushed-over hillsides, but we didn't see any hogs moving.

Heading deeper into the area we continued to probe for pigs, trying small one-man drives, tossing rocks into likely-looking pockets--the usual tricks. Nothing worked until about 4:00 p.m., when one of our drives got a small group of hogs racing around some unbelievably thick brush. I was the driver, and at the sound of pigs running I hit the thicket like a fullback. My reward was the sound of my partner's rifle echoing off the canyon walls. I knew he had a hog down.

Despite the fact that we had agreed beforehand not to do this, he had gone and done it--shot a monstrous boar, a hog that had to weigh near 300 pounds on the hoof. I remember slumping to the

It's become almost impossible for an outsider to obtain permission to hunt private land for hogs these days. The solution, if you're up to it, is to tackle nearby public land.

ground in near exhaustion, the corners of my mouth turned down in a sort of half scowl. Soon the thrill of taking a public land pig passed from his face, and he sat beside me. "Now you've done it," I remember saying (along with a couple of unprintable expletives). "You couldn't take one of the little sows, you had to go and shoot this horrible thing!"

It was then it hit him, too. We shot it, now we were responsible for lugging it back to the truck. The truck was all the way to China.

We got that old boar boned out in an hour or so, and were on the way back by 5:30 p.m.. The sun went down about 7:00 p.m., and there was no moon. With mini-flashlights we humped up the mountainside on overgrown deer trails, one of us slipping or falling down every 15 minutes or so. By the time we got back to the vehicle it was almost 10:00 p.m. My pants didn't have any knees left, my face and arms were scratched as if I had been in a cat fight, and my rifle sported two beautiful new dings. My partner looked even worse. Two days later we both got the poison oak.

Admittedly, that was the worst public land wild boar hunt I've ever been on. I learned several lessons on that death march, not the

To find potential public land hot spots, obtain BLM, U.S. Forest Service, and topographical maps, studying them for water and cover close to private grain fields. Maps can also show you access corridors into vast tracts of public acreage.

Public land hog hunting is flat hard work, with the best hunting found far from roads. If you are ready to meet the challenge and bust the brush, you might discover your own unhunted hot spots.

least of which is simply not to shoot a monster hog just before dark that far from the vehicle in that nasty an area. Believe it or not, my regular hunting partners and I have passed up big boars more than once that we could have easily taken simply because the pack to the truck with all the meat would have been a worse experience than a tax audit. I remember one conversation that went something like this:

"Hey you guys! Look at the size of that big boar down there! Let's go!"

"What pig? Craig, do you see a boar down there? I think Durwood's eyes are getting bad."

"Bob, I can't see anything down there but brush. I think we'd do a lot better if we hunted back toward the truck the rest of the day."

"Precisely! Let's get out of this wasteland."

"Hey you guys! Are you nuts! There's a pig down there. Where are you going?!"

"C'mon, Durwood, we need to hunt where the light's better so you can see reality a little more clearly."

I've had my best public land success on steep, brush-choked hillsides dotted with small openings and water very close by. Craig Boddington now has the enviable task of backpacking this big sow four miles uphill to the truck. (Photo by Craig Boddington)

Such is the fate of the public land hog hunter. The sad truth about hunting wild boar in California today is that the hunting is a lot better--and a lot less physically demanding--on private ranches. The private ranches, generally speaking, have better habitat in terms of food and, especially, water, and they have much better vehicle access. That makes it easy to get into hog country and, more importantly, much easier to get the meat back to the cooler. The down side of private vs. public land hunting is, of course, the cost. You can hunt public land for free, while ranchers and guides will charge you for the privilege of hunting hogs on their property.

Chapters 7, 8, and 9 feature an in-depth look at hunting private ranches, hiring guides, and costs. Chapter 13 takes a look at the kind of gear a hog hunter needs, including the necessary tools to hunt public land backcountry areas efficiently. The remainder of this chapter will help you find public land areas up and down the state that offer you the best chances at bagging a wild boar.

However, before you decide to tackle a public land hog hunt, keep a few things in mind. First and foremost, the country is usually

Here's what you're looking for -- heavy cover, natural foods, a small water hole, and a well used trail. I found this spot at midday, set up an evening stand, and shot a nice meat sow that evening.

rough. You need to be in reasonable physical condition to take it on. The best hunting will be away from the roads, meaning you not only have to get there--on foot--but be physically able to get your meat out before it spoils. Most of this country is arid, with no potable water available. Be sure to carry enough to avoid dehydration. Pack some lightweight, high-energy food, like granola bars. A small first aid kit is a good idea, too. And before you head into these remote areas, tell someone else where you've gone and when you expect to be back, just in case.

A bonus to some of this public land poking around is the other hunting opportunities you will stumble across. For example, I've found some awfully good deer hunting in a couple of these areas (no, I won't tell which ones!). Most of the units have more than their share of quail and rabbits, and a serious varmint caller would be surprised at the number of coyotes and bobcats he'd find in a few of these places. I carry a small notebook and pen on my trips into remote areas, and make notes as to what I see. In one particular area during quail season my partners and I have been known to carry a single-shot, long-range scoped handgun in our pack frames along with a shotgun and a couple of boxes of shells. We go in hunting hogs, but as often as not the only reward is some fast and furious quail shooting. To me that's as much fun, and sure makes for an easier pack back to the truck.

Public Land Hot Spots

There are more wild hogs in central California than any other region of the state, and much of the better public land wild boar habitat is administered by Bureau of Land Management, P.O. Box 365, Hollister, CA 95024; phone (408) 637-8183. This office will provide you with general information on all the areas listed below. The Hollister office administers a total of 315,000 acres in the counties of Fresno, Merced, Monterey, Madera, and San Benito. Generally speaking, hunting pressure on areas with easy public access is high, and success rates low. As is the case with deer hunting, you'll consistently find more hogs away from easy access.

Laguna Mountain is one of the better areas for wild hog hunting. This 3000-acre parcel has only foot access, one reason it offers a reasonable chance for success. Vehicle access is from Coalinga Rd. in southern San Benito County. The BLM, California Department of Fish & Game, and San Benito County Fish and Game Commission have worked together in recent years to conduct a number of small controlled burns in the area for habitat improvement, and they have worked in terms of increased game numbers. The BLM land is completely surrounded by patrolled private property, and care must be taken to stay on the public side of the fence. United States Geological Survey (USGS) topographic maps are recommended; for this area, use the Hepsedam Peak and Lonoak maps. USGS maps are available from most mountaineering and large sporting goods stores, or by mail for $2.50 each from the Distribution Center, USGS, Federal Center, Denver, CO 80225.

In this same general area is what the locals refer to as the Sweetwater Springs BLM parcel. To reach the area, at King City take the First Street offramp off Highway 101 and proceed to Bitterwater Rd. Travel 14 1/2 miles to Highway 25, then turn northbound and go two miles to the intersection of Coalinga Rd. Turn left on Coalinga Rd. and follow the winding course until you determine on a good map where you should park (the small parking shoulder isn't marked as such on the map). The hunting area lies between Laguna and Tully mountains south of Coalinga Rd. The hike is straight uphill for two or three miles, then head straight down into the remote portions of the parcel. Once into the area the country opens up, and spot & stalk hunting is a good way to go. However, you need to carry water and be prepared to carry a hog back to the truck on a tough uphill climb. This is one of my favorite public land hog areas, and also holds good numbers of quail and some decent California mule deer bucks, too.

The Clear Creek Management Area is a 50,000-acre area that, unfortunately for hunters, is a popular spot for off-road vehicle users, rock hounds, and the like. Access is via Clear Creek Road off the Coalinga/Los Gatos Creek Road (it's called Coalinga Road in San Benito County and Los Gatos Road in Fresno County). There is also access off of New Idria Road four miles south of Idria. Clear Creek is a relatively popular place for deer, pig, and quail hunters. There are any number of roads and jeep trails that help users in the area spread out. The BLM does discourage use of the Clear Creek area when conditions are dry due to the health hazard resulting from the presence of serpentine rock formations and naturally-occurring asbestos in the soil, dust, and water found in the area. Most area use occurs after the first rains of fall. Clear Creek can be excellent at times for wild boar hunting, but you have to be willing to hike away from the roads and explore the deeper, brushy cuts and canyons. The Hollister BLM office can provide a good map of the area for around a dollar.

Condon Peak is another possibility is this area. Access to the several-thousand-acre-Condon Peak portion of the Clear Creek Management Area is possible on foot without traveling through the asbestos zone of Clear Creek. Vehicle access is at the Fresno/San Benito County line along Coalinga Road (San Benito County) or Los Gatos Road (Fresno County). It's a rugged area, and holds good numbers of deer and quail in addition to hogs. The BLM has been working with the state fish and game department to crush and burn

You'll find very little potable water on public land; be sure and carry plenty with you. Two public land hog hunters didn't a few years back near Coalinga, got lost, and died of dehydration in 100-degree-plus temperatures.

On public land you can't be picky -- you take the first hog you see, and be happy to have it. DFG biologist Don Pine was tickled with this spotted sow, whose off-color coat didn't affect the flavor of the meat one bit. (Photo by Durwood Hollis)

the brush in this area to improve habitat, an action that will only help hog populations in years to come. One hint: while backcountry areas are the best bet here, don't overlook the oak-studded ridges right near the parking lot. Where the oaks border heavy cover is a good spot at first and last light.

Stockdale Mountain is accessible by vehicle at the end of Slack Canyon Road northwest of Parkfield. The area is relatively small (2000 acres) but holds reasonable numbers of hogs at times, as well as deer and quail. The public access into the area is by foot only, and it's good to keep in mind that following a good rain the last five miles of Slack Canyon Road, which is dirt, is usually impassable. This is a heavily brushed-over area and difficult to hunt, but it can be productive. Surrounding private lands are posted, and maps are needed to keep you from crossing the line. The Stockdale Mountain and Smith Mountain USGS maps are what you need for this area.

Coalinga Mineral Springs is another area that is worth looking at when hunting wild boar. Vehicle access is located 18 miles west of

Coalinga by taking Highway 198, then following the Coalinga Mineral Springs Road to the end. The main access to the BLM lands here is through the Coalinga Mineral Springs Park, operated by Fresno County. No shooting is allowed in the park itself, but you can use the park to gain access to the BLM lands on either side. The area encompasses a little over 9000 acres, and also holds deer and quail. This is one steep, tough area, with deep brush-choked canyons and little in the way of "easy" terrain. A 2 1/2-mile hiking trail provides easy access to the top of Kreyenhagen Peak. This trail has been designated a National Recreation Trail due to its scenic quality. If you plan on camping in the park, call the Fresno County Parks Department during normal business hours prior to your arrival. You must bring your own water to this area, as no potable sources are available. A Sherman Peak USGS map will help you hunt this locale.

Williams Hill, found nine miles west of San Ardo on the Lockwood-San Ardo Rd., is a possibility, with several thousand acres of accessible public land available for hunting, with best access along the ridge tops. Hog hunting here is fair at best, with the better hunting in winter and spring following some good rains. The limiting factor in pig populations here is the lack of water during summer, though the BLM says that hog populations are increasing. There are quite a few deer and quail here. It's another area of tough country that demands a lot out of the hunter.

The Griswold Hills has a limited number of hogs, and some absolutely horrible country that will result in a tough pack out with any animal you harvest. Public access to the area is located off New Idria Road, just south of its intersection with Panoche Road. The BLM access is less than a quarter-mile wide off the road, so be alert for signs showing you the way. A Panoche USGS map will help. There is limited water here, and it is best hunted in late spring and early winter after it rains and hogs move in from across New Idria Road. Be advised that many of the dirt roads in the area are virtually impassable after a heavy rain.

Two other BLM areas here are worth mentioning, though both lack key habitat components (primarily water) for hogs to live there all year. They are Tumey Hills and the Panoche Hills. USGS maps are a must for these areas (Mercy Hot Springs and Chounet Ranch for the Panoche Hills, Tumey Hills and Monocline Ridge for Tumey Hills). Occasionally wild hogs will pass through the areas, but the big draw here is the excellent numbers of quail and the chance at a good buck deer. These are the kinds of areas I like to go into in late fall primarily hunting quail, but carrying a hog gun and pack frame "just in case."

Perhaps the best-known public land hunting area in all of coastal southern California, at least for deer and quail, is the huge 1,724,000-acre <u>Los Padres National Forest</u>, which includes the 165,000-acre Ventana Wilderness Area. The best wild boar hunting in the forest is found in Monterey, San Luis Obispo, and Santa Barbara counties, in that order. The terrain is, for the most part, brushy and steep, with only scattered permanent water sources. In the Monterey Ranger District there are 335 miles of maintained hiking trails, 130 primitive camp units, 12 campgrounds, and four beach picnic sites--lots of areas to begin a wild boar hunt. The better hog areas in this region include Skinner Ridge, Chew's Ridge, the upper Arroyo Seco area, Willow Creek, and Boucher's Gap. For the adventurous hunter who is willing and physically able to explore this area with a backpack, the rewards can be great not only in terms of hogs, but deer, quail, turkeys, and bandtail pigeons. The Monterey Ranger District, Los Padres National Forest, 406 Mildred, King City, CA 93930; phone (408) 385-5434 can give you more detailed information. Be sure and ask about the specific USGS maps needed to navigate forest backcountry areas.

Near San Luis Reservoir is the <u>Upper Cottonwood Wildlife Area</u>, a 4000-acre unit managed by the state department of fish & game. The area is located east of Gilroy and west of Los Banos off of Highway 152. The area is operated for hunting and similar activities, and special permits are needed for hog hunting and the opening weekend of deer season, with a very limited hog hunting season. Usually there are two hunts, an upper unit hunt with 25 permits, and a lower unit hunt with 10 permits, with hunting taking place in May and June. It is very possible to take a hog on one of these permit hunts if you work at it. For information contact the California Department of Fish & Game, 18110 West Henry Miller Rd., Los Banos, CA 93635; phone (209)826-0463.

Public land hogs are taken out on the hunter's back, pure and simple. On short hikes, you might carry a small pig out just gutted. A better idea is to bone the animal, carrying out only meat.

Further north, the Bureau of Land Management office in Ukiah administers hundreds of thousands of acres of public land, much of which offers the public land pig hunter a reasonable chance of success. General information, maps, etc., can be had from the district office, 555 Leslie St., Ukiah, CA 95482; phone (707) 462-3873. The district office can also recommend specific USGS topographic maps that will be very helpful in hunting the region.

The most popular and productive hog area in this district is the <u>Cow Mountain Recreation Area</u>, located only five miles from downtown Ukiah. This area stretches over 50,000 acres, and is a very good deer hunting area. I hunted deer here on a regular basis back in the early and mid-1970's, when I was a student at Sacramento State University, and shot a buck every season. Generally speaking, the country is steep and heavily brushed-over, making it tough to use spot-and-stalk tactics on hogs. Throughout the area, the use of dogs is very popular, and without a doubt the most successful overall method of hog hunting. No matter what method of hunting you employ, pigs seem to prefer an oak-grassland habitat adjacent to thick escape cover.

The best hunting in the Cow Mountain unit is in the northern half, where vehicle access is restricted to the main road only. The southern portion, around Red Mountain, is a popular off-road area frequented by dirt bikes, four-wheel drive trucks, and other types of ATVs, and these vehicles can travel any road they like. In the northern tier, hog hunters have their best success hiking up the McClure, Sulphur, and North Fork Mill Creek drainages. This is steep, tough country, and best hunting occurs in spring and fall, when the weather is cooler than the blistering daytime heat of summer. The Forty Acre opening, a grassy meadow, is a good spot to glass at first light. One caution: a large portion of this area is owned by the Cow Mountain Hunting Club, and access is restricted. The Ukiah BLM office can help you mark the boundaries on your maps.

A 20,000-acre parcel of the Cow Mountain unit burned fairly completely back in 1981, forcing hogs out of that area. However, as vegetation grows back the pigs will return. This is an area I'd seriously consider for both hog and deer hunting right now.

The Walker Ridge, a 50,000-acre parcel, and Knoxville area, encompassing 25,000 acres, also hold decent numbers of wild boar. Along Walker Ridge/Omdoam Valley area, on the Lake/Colusa county line, some 40,000 acres of public land offer good hunting for wild boar. However, it is drier than the aforementioned creek drainages and doesn't contain as much oak-grassland habitat. The Ukiah BLM office reports that several hunters in recent years have reported seeing wild hogs foraging on the young green plants growing in the bed of the low Indian Valley Reservoir. Several years of below-normal rainfall have dropped the lake level, and the pigs have moved into the area. Other productive hog hunting areas in the Walker Ridge region include Cold Springs Canyon (located just north of the Blue Lake campground); the Cold Springs area around Wintun Campground; and Grapevine Flat, just west of the Barrel Spring campground. All three of these areas feature the essential foraging grounds wild hogs love (wet meadow areas on grassy hillsides,) and they can often be spotted rooting at first or last light. Access to Walker Ridge is via State Highway 20 to the Walker Ridge

The "Hog Hotel" is the largest bed Durwood Hollis and I have ever found. It held two dozen hogs when we first stumbled into it. Traditional use areas like this are the places you go back to time and time again on public land.

turn-off, or from the Bartlett Springs turn-off on Highway 20 at Nice, or through the Wilbur Springs turn-off east of Walker Ridge.

The Knoxville parcel is accessible from Morgan Valley Road in Lower Lake or from the Knoxville-Berryessa Road from Lake Berryessa. The Devilshead Road turn-off provides access to the major blocks of public land in this area. The turn-off is marked with a sign, and is approximately one mile east of the Homestake Mining Company's mine site.

The Cache Creek area is also a reasonable bet for wild boar hunting in this region. Access is adjacent to Highway 20 and is just eight miles north of Clearlake Oaks. The access is limited to horses and foot traffic only, with no motor vehicles permitted past the parking lot. In addition, this is one area where dogs are not permitted to hunt mammals, giving the pigs a haven free from both vehicles and houndsmen. There are a few scattered private land holdings in the area, and a USGS topographic map with them marked should be carried to avoid trespassing. Hunt Cache Creek itself, or hike beyond the Baton Flat campground and explore Deadman Canyon, Rocky Creek, and the foothills surrounding the Wilson Valley area.

The California Department of Fish & Game periodically holds a special wild boar hunt around <u>Lake Sonoma</u>, located west of Healdsburg. This 3000 acre tract of public land is surrounded by excellent private land hog habitat, and when the state offers a hunt it's worth applying for. The rules change, and information on current hunting status can be obtained by writing Lake Sonoma Pig Hunt, California Department of Fish & Game, P.O. Box 47, Yountville, CA 94599; phone (707) 944-2011. Hunting occurs from November through April, and separate archery and gun hunts are offered.

Another state-operated hunting program that theoretically offers a chance at wild hogs is held on the <u>Tehama Wildlife Area</u> located near Red Bluff and forming part of the northern border of the popular Dye Creek Preserve. This area encompasses 44,000 acres, with wild hog hunting allowed by special permit on four units: Grapevine/Cottonwood Creek (7350 acres); Little Antelope (8650 acres); Upper Dye Creek (2537 acres); and DeWitt (2524 acres). Weekend-only hunting is permitted in November, April, and May. However, hog hunting here is generally poor. If you're going to come, apply for the opening weekend of each hunting period and hope for the best. For more information, write the DFG, 601 Locust St., Redding, CA 96001; phone (916) 225-2300.

The wild boar continues to expand its range up and down the state. As it does so, new public land areas will begin to hold huntable numbers of hogs. Public land hunting will never rival private ranch hunting in terms of simplicity or success rates, but for those willing to put in their time and work hard at it, the successes will come. And believe me, while I thoroughly enjoy hunting private property with guides and all the amenities that go with it, no hog tastes as sweet as one I've taken the hard way--with a backpack on public land, hunting with one or two of my best friends.

CHAPTER 7

MILITARY BASE HUNTING

It was the first weekend in almost a month that I didn't have any pressing obligations, and the itch to go hunting just had to be scratched. And as I hiked along the oak-grassland countryside my spirits soared, even though it was already Sunday afternoon and I hadn't seen any hogs yet.

Two hours before dark I set up a glassing station under the shade of an old oak and began picking apart a nearby brush-choked hillside. In the distance a rifle shot broke the silence for a moment, then all was quiet again. It was hard to imagine that before dawn the next day this tranquil piece of real estate would be transformed from a public hunting area into a frenetic scene of mock battle complete with tanks, attack helicopters, and armored troop carriers.

This was my second wild boar hunting trip onto massive Fort Hunter Liggett. I hadn't taken a hog on that first expedition, but it had given me a feel for the base and an idea of where I wanted to be next time. I was there now, patiently waiting out the end of the day and hoping a hog would feed into an opening in the thick brush.

It was the calling of a lone valley quail that turned my attention to the left. There, moving carefully through a small open pocket in the thick chaparral was the dark body of a hog. It was working its way down the ridgeline heading for water, and I hopped up and trotted ahead to get a better vantage point. Settling down under another oak, I placed my pack frame in front of me to use as a bench to rest my rifle. It was only a minute or two later that the hog moved into another small opening and I squeezed the trigger of my battered old .30-06. Ten minutes later I was beginning a labor of love--field dressing a fat meat sow of 150 pounds or so. The grind back to the truck was rather satisfying, despite the boned-out carcass and empty canteen.

Fort Hunter Liggett is one of two military bases in California open to hunting on a limited basis in California, and by far the better of the two for hog hunting. (Camp Roberts is the other, discussed later in this chapter). It has become one of the most popular public hunting areas in the state's central coast region, for several reasons. First and foremost, it isn't like hunting a wasteland. You can harvest not only wild boar, but deer, quail, bandtail pigeons, rabbits, tree squirrels, and waterfowl in season. As this book is being written, the base is planning to allow a limited number of wild turkey hunters in the spring of 1990, a first.

Also important to many is the ease of access to the base. You don't have to be a mountain climber, study dozens of confusing maps, or camp in desolate, waterless, mosquito-infested backcountry hell holes to have a chance at a successful hunt. At Hunter Liggett, you simply report in at the check station and go hunting. More on the exact procedures in a moment.

Another important factor is the cost. In addition to your California hunting license, a wild boar hunter must pay only $12 for a one-day permit, $18 for a two-day permit, or $55 for a civilian annual permit to hunt on the base. There are no ups, no extras, no other costs. The hunt fees even allow you to bring along one non-hunting visitor free of charge.

Fort Hunter Liggett comprises some 165,000 acres of land on the inland side of the Santa Lucia mountain range in central California, about 20 miles southwest of King City. The Los Padres National Forest butts up against the base on the west, with private holdings controlling the eastern border.

Existing wildlife habitat on the base has been improved to the benefit of the native game animals thanks to the combined efforts of the U.S. Army and the California Department of Fish & Game. In fact, wildlife habitat projects completed in the past five years have directly resulted in improved hunter success, according to Bob

For the 1989 season, Fort Hunter Liggett built a large new wildlife check station. Hunters are required to check in and out here, as well as check any game they may have taken.

Decker, a biologist hired by the army a few years ago to manage wildlife and habitat on the post.

Mother Nature did not go out of her way to make a hunter's job an easy one on the base. The reservation's steep ravines, brush-choked canyons, chaparral-covered mountains, and oak-grassland foothills are tough to cover on foot, and even tougher to see hogs in. There are numerous creeks and small ponds on the base, too, making staking out a water hole a chancy bet for the pig hunter. It's tough hunting, to be sure, and hunter success rates are not all that high. Still, the hogs are here and just like in all other public land hunting, those who pay their dues, learn the lay of the land, and stick with it have a relatively good chance at finding pigs.

Fort Hunter Liggett is open to hunting on weekends and federal holidays when military training schedules permit. The hunting program is administered from the Wildlife Check Station, located on Mission Creek Road just inside the main gate. Beginning each Tuesday at 4:30 p.m., a list of specific training areas which may be used for hunting on the coming weekend is recorded on telephone number (408) 385-1205. Reservations for weekend hunting are taken beginning on the Wednesday before the coming weekend or holiday. General public reservations are accepted from noon until 4:30 p.m., and you can make a reservation by calling (408) 385-1205. Up to four reservations may be made per phone call. Walk-in reservations are not accepted.

When calling to make a hunting reservation, be sure to have the specific area you wish to hunt and the day(s) you want to hunt ready for the reservationist. Also have the name and California hunting license number of each person in your party.

On hunting days, any reservations not claimed by 7:00 a.m. will be canceled and handed out on a first-come, first-serve basis. Before going hunting, all sportsmen are required to check in at the Wildlife Check Station, as well as check out before leaving the post. Hunters may also change hunting areas if they check first at the Check Station, and the new area they wish to hunt is open and space available.

If you take a hog on the post (or any game animal) you must check it in at the Check Station. As a service to hunters, a cold locker is available to store your game for the day for a $2.00 fee. Keep in mind that all California state game laws and regulations apply while hunting on the post, and there are several military and state game wardens patrolling the base at any given time.

The only difference between state and base hog hunting regulations is the open season. Hog hunting is permitted here only between the end of October and April 1.

Hog hunting is an up-and-down affair on Fort Hunter Liggett, with the availability of food and water a big factor in determining hunter success. During the 1988-89 season, only 29 hogs were checked through the Wildlife Check Station (in contrast, 179 buck and 180 antlerless deer were taken on the post). Eight of the 29 hogs were taken in area 10/13, with four each harvested in areas 9 and 16. Three hogs were taken in area 7, while two hogs each were shot in areas 2, 6, 24, and 27. One hog each was killed in areas 3 and 29. Year in and year out, these are the better hog areas on the base. If I were to hunt an area that didn't produce a hog in 1988-89, it would either

A good way to hunt on Fort Hunter Liggett is to hike a short ways off a dirt road, climb to a good vantage point, and wait. Even if you don't spot any hogs, other hunters will often push animals past your look-out.

be area 5 or area 25. Both have produced hogs in the past, and have good pig habitat. The largest hogs on the base seem to come from areas 10/13, 9 and 16, as a rule.

While the hunting season opens in October, the best wild boar hunting on the post usually occurs during the cooler months of January and February. All weapon types are legal for wild boar hunting here, though there are some restrictions regarding what handgun calibers are legal. By and large, however, Fort Hunter Liggett is a rifleman's hunting ground.

You'll find the people at the Wildlife Check Station helpful and friendly. To obtain a packet with post map, season dates, hunting rules, fees, and reservation information, send a self-addressed, stamped envelope to Outdoor Recreation Branch, Hg. 7th Infantry Division and Fort Ord, Fort Ord, CA 93941.

Camp Roberts is the other military base Californians should consider as a viable public hunting ground. Located west of Highway 101 between Paso Robles and King City, Camp Roberts allows civilians onto the base each year to hunt wild boar and deer. The base

Camp Roberts features very open terrain, and the best boar hunting is opening weekend. Expect moving animals and some long shooting, but the potential to take a good hog is there.

is primarily an oak-grassland country, with some thick brushy areas and water relatively prevalent in several small ponds and the Nacimiento River, which runs through the center of the post.

Opening weekend is a reservation-only situation, as all available spaces are usually full. Opening weekend for both deer and wild boar hunting is usually set for the last weekend of August. Written applications are required to reserve an opening day spot, which is held August 1. However, getting on post to hunt after opening weekend is usually not a problem.

For hog hunters, opening weekend is definitely the best time to be here. Much of the post consists of open terrain, and there is excellent hog habitat surrounding the base on private land. After the first weekend or two, most of the hogs on the post have been driven off into this neighboring private property.

That isn't to say that you can't take a hog here throughout the hunting season. It's always better to be lucky than good, and you'll need a healthy dose of luck here. But the competition will be light, and the experience a good one.

Be sure and bring your pack frame on military base hunts. More than likely, any hogs you harvest will come off the roads, making getting them back to the vehicle a chore.

As is the case on Fort Hunter Liggett, Camp Roberts has some severe restrictions in terms of access in and out of the base, closed areas, etc. For example, hunting areas 6 and 7 are closed to all weapons except shotguns and muzzleloaders due to their close proximity to Highway 101. All big-game hunters are required to wear blaze orange hats or vests. And all hunters are required to check in and out of the Wildlife Check Station whether successful or not. It's located just off Highway 101 at the East Garrison entrance to the base.

Hunting fees are reasonable, just $8.00 per day or $30.00 per season for hunters over 16 years of age. In addition to deer and wild boar, doves may be hunted here from September 1-4, and quail and rabbits are fair game in season.

For more information on Camp Roberts, a base map, regulations, and opening weekend application forms, write Department of Fish and Game, Camp Roberts Wildlife Program, P.O. Box 6360, Los Osos, CA 93412. A recorded message phone can be called at (805) 238-8167.

CHAPTER 8

HIRING A GUIDE

When I was a lot younger and a bit more starry-eyed, I used to sift through the back pages of the popular outdoor magazines and dream about going on a fully-guided hunt someday. I had visions of top-quality camps, guides who knew elk and deer and bears better than I new my folks, equipment that never broke down, and no shortage of game. Hire a guide, I thought, pay the money, and I was virtually assured of shooting the trophy of a lifetime.

I'm a lot older now, and I've made more than my share of fully-guided hunting and fishing trips all over the world. As Editor of both Petersen's BOWHUNTING and FISHING magazines and a Feature Editor for Petersen's HUNTING magazine, I've been invited to share guides' camps from Alaska to Africa, California to Canada, Scandinavia to Spain, Montana to Mexico. What I've seen has opened my eyes up to the world of guides and outfitters, and fully-guided hunts.

I should begin by saying that the majority of the guides I've hunted with over the years have been pretty darn good. Most are honest, hard-working individuals who give you good value for your money. And then there are the bad apples, the few who give guiding a bad name. These are rip-off artists who will promise you the moon--until they get your money and get you into camp. That's when you find that the actual "guides" are really college kids who've hunted less than you, and the outfitter is really a glorified salesman

Hunting with a good guide is an excellent idea if you want to use your handgun, as they'll have access to property holding enough animals to let you stalk very close to one. Cliff Sebasto guided Lyle Dorey to this good boar on the Work Ranch.

who knows more about fast talk and how to get the cork out of a bottle than how to find game. His horses are lame, the food's worse than a greasy spoon on a bad day, and the game was shot out five years ago. Nothing can sour you on hunting any faster than these kinds of snake oil salesmen. My very first guided hunt was almost a disaster. I booked a 10-day elk and deer combination hunt in Idaho's rugged Selway-Bitterroot Wilderness Area with an outfitter who had been around for a while. There were several hunters in the crew he was taking in, but he dropped two hunters each at three different camps several miles apart.

Fortunately the outfitter himself guided my partner and I, while two very inexperienced guides handled the other camps. Things went very well, and my partner and I shot two bulls in the same spot that came to the bugle the second day of the hunt. One, a big 6x6 that scored 330 Boone & Crockett points, was the largest I ever took until a few seasons ago. As they say in elk hunting, the fun's over when you pull the trigger, as we were about to find out.

One reason for hiring the services of a guide is that they will have permission to hunt the best private ranches, as well as know where the hogs are and how they move.

It was a seven-hour hike from camp to the carcasses and back each day, and it took a full five days to get all the meat down to camp plus the hide of a big black bear we shot feeding on one of the carcasses one day. The outfitter disappeared after the first day of packing meat, saying he had to check on his other camps, and I spent the rest of my hunt boning and packing meat instead of hunting deer. It was my first guided hunt, and I didn't know any better. I thought this was the way it was supposed to go. After all, I wasn't afraid of hard work, and I wanted to help with camp chores and such. Besides, I had shot one helluva big bull, and that made everything all right, in my mind.

It wasn't until later that I found out that the outfitter had a close relationship with Jim Beam, and that on virtually all fully-guided hunts like this he should have had camp help to take care of the meat packing chores while he took us deer hunting. The other two camps of two hunters each shot one small bull between them, in no small part thanks to young guides who had little, if any, experience.

All this is a roundabout way of saying that there are lots of wild boar guides in California today. Most of them are as honest as the day is long, have permission to hunt on several different pieces of private property, monitor the movement of the game closely, and will give you an excellent hunt for your dollar. There are many, however, who are less than honest and will rip you off. It's up to you to sift through the brochures and hype and pick a guide, if you want to go on a guided hunt. As the saying goes, "Let the buyer beware. You pays your money, you takes your chances."

An example is a guide who operated on the central coast some years back. He advertised guaranteed success on Russian Imperial boar, huge hogs that weighed 500, 600, 700 pounds or more. All this became a little suspicious to a friend of mine, an outdoor writer on one of the state's leading newspapers, and with the help of the Department of Fish and Game they set up a little "sting" operation. When the dust settled they found that this so-called "guide" was actually buying hogs at auction in the San Joaquin Valley, trucking them to his "hunting" area and, after taking his clients on a simulated walk through the woods, having an assistant open the pens and letting his unsuspecting hunters shoot these huge pigs. The giveaway was the floppy ears, curly tails, and the ear tags found in his broken-down truck.

There's not too much of that going on today, as far as I can tell. But to make sure you avoid this kind of heartbreak and rip-off, it will pay to thoroughly check out a guide's credentials before you send him any money and actually book a hunt.

Guides vs. Private Ranchers

In this chapter we are concerned only with guides, and not with private ranchers who hunt their own property. These kinds of ranch hunts will be discussed at length in Chapter 9. For our purposes, a guide is defined as someone who is paid by clients to take them hunting on property he does not own. This can be either private property or public land, though it is the rare guide indeed who takes clients pig hunting on anything but private ground.

Most guides who take sportsmen out on private ranches have an agreement with the landowner that has the guide pay the property

Here's what a good guide can do for you--put you within point-blank range of a big bruiser of a hog that doesn't even know you're in the neighborhood. This is the spot we all want to be in.

owner a fee for every hunter he brings onto the property, or for every hog he kills. Most guides pay for every hog they kill, and generally speaking that is in the $100 to $150 range, though it may be more or less. This is a sort of trespass fee that comes out the fees you pay the guide for the hunt. They should also have written permission from the landowner to guide on the property, although because many guides are local fellows who grew up with the ranchers written agreements really aren't necessary for them to do business comfortably together. I like my guides to have one, just because there are a few who like to fudge a bit on property boundaries when the hunting gets tough. I don't want to be in a position of having a trespass ticket slapped on me unknowingly.

How to Choose a Guide

Before you decide on a specific guide and send them money, you should first decide exactly what it is that you expect for your hard-earned dollars. A quality hunting experience is not something you can put your finger on, but rather a state of mind that varies from individual to individual. For some a quality hunt may mean driving around in a 4X4, drinking coffee and telling stories, little physical effort, and an easy meat pig. For others it might mean pulling on a pack frame and heading out afoot, carrying your game back to the vehicle on your back. Some like to follow hounds as they chase hogs through heavy brush, while others don't like hunting with dogs at all. The best way to ensure satisfaction is to match your wants and desires to your guide's method of hunting.

To do that you need to ask questions. Don't be afraid to ask too many questions, either. The worst thing that can happen is to have a misunderstanding between you and your guide that will affect the quality of your time together. The better guides want you to both have an enjoyable day and shoot a hog. Let them know what you expect, and let them tell you what they can offer in terms of services, prices, and more. Only after all your questions have been answered to your satisfaction should you book.

The first thing to do is to write or call many different guides and ranches offering hog hunts. Many of you have friends who have already had a good guided hunting experience. Call your friends and ask them several pointed questions about the hunt. Appendix A at the end of this book lists several guides, together with answering many of the questions you will want to ask before booking. Ask for their current brochures and price lists, read them carefully, then make a few telephone calls. Ask your questions, write down the answers, and when you're all through you'll be in a position to make an intelligent choice.

What questions do you ask? Here are the 25 questions that I want answered before I book any hunt.

1) How much does a hunt cost for a meat pig? A trophy boar?

2) What is your definition of a trophy boar? Tooth length? Animal weight? The definition of a meat pig?

3) If I book for a trophy boar hunt and don't take a "trophy", but a meat hog instead, do I still have to pay the trophy fee? What if I don't get a shot at a trophy boar at all?

4) If I shoot and miss, does that mean I still have to pay the full hunt cost? If I don't kill a pig, do I pay the full fee?

5) What are the "hidden" costs? Is there a charge to field dress the animal? Store it until I leave? Cape a trophy out for mounting?

6) What's the hunt duration? If I kill my hog before the end of the time period, is the hunt then over, or can I ride around and enjoy the scenery, take photographs, etc.?

7) What about lodging? Am I on my own? Do you have any available? If so, does that cost extra?

8) Is food and drink provided? If so, at what cost? Can I provide my own food?

9) Can I bring a non-hunting guest along, like my wife or son? If so, does this cost extra?

10) How do you hunt? By vehicle? On foot? Will I be expected to be able to hike all day in steep terrain?

11) What gear do I need, besides my weapon--binoculars, rain gear, heavy coat, good boots, knife, etc.?

12) What weapons do you allow? Rifles? Bow and arrow? Muzzleloaders? Handguns? Shotguns with slugs? What kinds of calibers and ammunition do you recommend?

13) Do you have a local taxidermist you recommend? Will you deliver my cape and skull there for me? If so, does that cost extra?

14) Is there a local butcher shop you recommend? Will they ship my meat to me, if I need it shipped?

15) Do you hunt public land, or private ground?

16) What's your success rate over the past two years?

17) How long have you been in the hog guiding business?

18) Do you have any references from past clients that I can call about your operation?

19) What kind of vehicles do you hunt from? Are all passengers in an enclosed cab, or do some have to ride in the back of an open pickup? Will I need a heavy coat for this? Is there a rifle rack, or do I need soft case for my weapon?

20) Is there a place I can park my motor home, or pitch a tent, if I want to camp this way?

21) Are you licensed and bonded? Have a current guide's license with the state? Insured?

22) Describe a typical hunting day to me. What time do we go out? Break for lunch? End in the evening?

When spot-and-stalk hunting doesn't produce, guides often know where hogs bed, allowing them to organize a successful drive. Chris Dorsey's big boar was the result of such a drive on the Work Ranch.

23) Will there be other hunters along besides my party? What's the maximum that will be hunting in our area at any one time?

24) Exactly where do we meet, and at what time? Will you send me a map with exact directions so I won't get lost?

25) If the weather's bad--rain, heavy fog, etc.--do we still hunt, or do I get a rain check?

References are very important sources of information. Spend a little time and a few dollars on the long-distance bill and call several, asking for their feel of the hunt and the guide. References will give you an insight into the operation that the guide can't. I shy away from guides who won't give references out, assuming that there must be something wrong, even if there isn't.

When talking with the guide, be sure you get a telephone number where he can be reached should problems arise (you're going to be late, for example). Give him your telephone number so he can call you if last minute problems pop up on his end, too.

Should you should expect to see dozens of hogs on a guided hunt? Ask this question of a guide before you book. Get all the details squared away before the hunt begins to avoid confusion and disappointment.

Communication is the Key

Honest, open communication between the hunter and his guide is the key to a successful, enjoyable guided hunt. So far we've talked about what you need to know about your guide. Equally important are the things your guide will expect from you.

I've talked with guides all over the world about the guide/client relationship, and it's amazing to note that no matter where they hunt or the game they pursue, their feelings are the same. Problem hunters cause as many, if not more, trouble than bad guides.

Probably the worst offense are hunters that don't listen to what the guide tells them, or don't do exactly what he tells them to do. When you hire a guide, you're hiring his expertise. You're foolish not to use it. If he tells you to shoot that hog right now, don't hesitate--shoot it before it figures out you're in the neighborhood, and the opportunity goes away. If the guide tells you to sit in a certain spot and not to move, don't get up and wander off. About the time

Muzzleloading hunters should seriously consider a guided hunt on good private property, where there are plenty of animals and a good chance of closing the range. Bob Sarber, left, and guide Tom Willoughby show what a muzzleloader can do.

you do is when the pigs will come by. If he tells you to shut up and quit talking, cut the chatter.

Guides always complain about their clients' lack of expertise with their weapon. You hear new horror stories every trip about the hunters who can't shoot, who can't take a rest quickly, who don't even know how to load their rifle, much less use it. If a guide puts you within reasonable range of a hog, and you have the time to make the shot--and don't--it's not his fault. He's done his job, and you should expect to pay for the hunt if you end up not taking a pig at all.

Most guides are also very nervous about when you put a round in the chamber. I can't blame them. They're usually in front of you when you're walking, and I get awfully nervous when a stranger is behind me with a .30-06. I don't want a round in the chamber until I tell him to put one there. You also hear about clients who have shot through the floorboards of the truck, who swore their rifle wasn't loaded--until it went off--or who have the wrong caliber ammunition for their rifle. The list goes on and on. Let the guide dictate how the firearms are handled. Have the courtesy to show him the weapon is unloaded before entering the vehicle or crossing a fence. Safety cannot be overemphasized.

Guided hunts can be the best hunting experience you'll ever have, or the worst. Do your homework, choose a guide that you feel comfortable with and who hunts the way you want to hunt, and you'll have a quality trip with an excellent chance of bringing home the bacon. Compared with the cost of hunting deer and other game throughout the West, a guided wild boar hunt in California is one of the most reasonably-priced hunting trips anywhere, and the chances for success are near 100 percent. At between $300 and $500, most fully-guided hog hunts cost only one-tenth of what similar deer and elk hunts throughout the West do.

For the first-time hog hunter, going with a knowledgeable guide will not only substantially increase your odds for success, but also teach you much about hog behavior. This knowledge can be used later on public land hunts. For an experienced sportsman, a fully-guided hunt is a way to avoid the back-breaking work often necessary for success on public land, as well as enjoy a relaxing weekend afield with good company. There's much to recommend a guided wild boar hunt with all the trimmings. Just be sure you do your homework and choose a guide that's right for your temperament and hunting style.

CHAPTER 9

RANCH HUNTS

In Chapter 8 we talked about guides who hunt other people's property or public land. In this chapter we'll deal only with hunting on private ranches that run their own hunting program.

If you're considering booking a ranch hunt, reading Chapter 7 carefully is a good idea, because many of the same things apply here. Booking a ranch hunt is really no different than booking with a guide, except that the question of where you'll be hunting and permission to hunt that property are already understood. You should, however, make a few phone calls to several ranches and ask the same basic questions that you do of guides. Get a reference list and call the people on it. Get everything understood before you send a check (I prefer agreements in writing).

When questioning someone who runs a ranch operation, you might want to be a bit more specific in terms of meals, lodging, camping, meat care, and so on. Many private ranches have built walk-in cold boxes designed specifically to keep your meat cool until it's time to head for home. Ask about this. Are meals and lodging included in the hunt price, or is that extra? One ranch I know, for example, charges basically the same rate for both meat hogs and trophy boars as others in the area, yet they charge clients extra each day for use of the ranch house for sleeping and a shower, and more money still each day they want meals. On a weekend hunt, that adds another $200 or so to the total cost, or roughly two-thirds the price of a meat hog. The accommodations and food are both very good, but you may not be willing to pay for this privilege and instead book

Frank Barotti, right, has been hunting with Craig Rossier at Camp 5 for some time, and his regular patronage paid off when Craig showed him this huge boar. The same can happen for you on a quality private ranch hunt. (Photo by Durwood Hollis)

somewhere else. The decision is yours, but one you can't make without all the facts in front of you.

What are the advantages of booking a ranch hunt instead of hiring a guide? There are a few, but these are little things that the one-time hunter may never notice and probably won't affect your chances of success, since both the better ranches and guides produce near 100 percent success rates for meat hogs, and better than 50 percent on trophy-class boars. However, many ranches have enrolled in California's Private Lands Management Program. This allows the rancher to set seasons and bag limits on a variety of game different from the state's general seasons, as long as they are approved by the California Department of Fish and Game. Most ranchers enroll in this program so that they can hold deer seasons later in the year than the general deer seasons of California, but there are other advantages.

Barley is like candy to a wild hog, acting like a magnet to draw and hold them in the area. Along the central coast that's just what most ranches plant. Hunting this type of country is part of what you pay for.

In exchange for this privilege, the ranchers are required to improve wildlife habitat substantially. This may include projects like building new water sources, planting food crops that wildlife (not cattle or sheep) prefer, conducting controlled burns, and so on. The end result is a large tract of land that is now a paradise for wildlife-- and in good pig country, that means, literally, "hog heaven."

In the central coast region, where barley and wheat farming is big business but natural water sources for wildlife are scarce, habitat improvements have contributed heavily to an increased population of wild boar. The hogs love to eat the grain, and they migrate to and from the fields to bedding areas in habitat-enriched locations on many private ranches. They stay in these areas because of the food and cover, to be sure, but the big draw is water, especially in years of drought or the hot summer months. As we've seen, wild hogs water every day if they can, and with a steady supply they'll not leave an area unless severely pressured.

When grain crops have been harvested, the hogs will gorge themselves on acorns, berries, bugs, and who-knows-what on these

Although it doesn't happen every time, on the better private ranches it isn't unusual to see hundreds of wild hogs in a single morning or evening. Those densities just don't exist on public land. (Photo by Durwood Hollis)

private ranches. These foods are readily available, in many cases, because of habitat improvements ranchers made on their property.

To the hunter, that means a couple of things. First, on these private ranches there will be a good pig population 365 days a year. That means that you can expect reasonably good hunting any time you want to go. Second, the ranchers will know just where to find the hogs on any given day, depending on the season, the weather, available food and water, and local hunting pressure. And third, the rancher won't pound on one small pocket of pigs unmercifully, shooting at them until they leave the ranch completely. He'll not overhunt bedding areas and the more popular travel routes on his ranch so as to not send the hogs off to another ranch. Many set aside small sanctuary areas where little if any hunting is permitted, giving the pigs a place to rest unmolested.

There are the side benefits of hunting a ranch, too. If you're a steady client on a particular ranch, for example, and have finally decided that next time you really want to take a big trophy boar for

Ranchers know the movement patterns of their hogs, and can set you up on a good stand overlooking well-used trails. This "hog highway" on Camp 5 is 16 inches wide from years of constant use.

the wall, you might call up the rancher and tell him so. Tell him that if he keeps his eye out for you and gives you a call as soon as he spots the kind of pig you want you'll be up that weekend. If he's smart he'll babysit that pig for you and put you on him as soon as you arrive. You might tip him a little extra, or pass along a bottle of Kentucky's finest after the hunt is over, to show your appreciation. But what he's doing is showing you that you're a valuable client, he appreciates your business, and wants to keep it. It's a good deal for everyone.

Private ranchers may also offer other types of hunting that you're interested in, hunting that goes first to his good customers. Many ranches have a few deer permits available each year, and most offer dove and quail shooting as well. A few are beginning to plant and release pheasants, and a few also offer exotic big game like Barbary sheep, Catalina goats, and the like. Hunting familiar ground is always more pleasant than hunting new property, and hunting it with the friends you've made on a private ranch can be doubly fun. Of course, in some cases this also holds true with guides.

The best ranch guides have all the ancillary equipment you need, like spotting scopes, to help ensure your success. They want you to enjoy yourself and take the kind of pig you want, so you'll come back again.

A typical day of hunting on a private ranch might go something like this. Hunters are up and about an hour or so before daylight, dressed and ready to go. There's a fresh pot of coffee on, and perhaps a few sweet rolls to take the edge off. Thermos bottles are filled, strategies discussed, and last-minute bets and heckling take place between the clients. Then off you go, heading for an area that the rancher knows will have hogs on this morning. Some of the party, if not all, fill out, and you're back at the ranch house by 10:00 a.m., ready for breakfast, which turns out to be a full-blown meal of eggs, sausage, ham, biscuits, fruit, juice, and coffee. While the guides skin, butcher, and hang the meat in the cool box, hunters take a nap or relax and enjoy the day. An evening hunt is organized, and a few hours before sundown you're back at it again. More of the party fill out, and you come back to a hearty supper of grilled steaks, baked potatoes, salad, garlic bread, and a good local bottle of wine. The next day? Up again, and those who didn't fill the day before have their hogs down before breakfast.

Many private ranches have built refrigerated meat storage lockers and cleaning areas, to help keep your hog clean and fresh prior to the trip home. These facilities really pay off in hot weather.

Appendix A lists several private ranches (and guides) that conduct their own hunting operations. Remember that the personalities of a piece of ranch land can vary as widely as the personalities of the landowner and his guides. Contact several ranches, get their brochures, and make some phone calls before booking a hunt to ensure that you'll not only be hunting property with plenty of pigs, but hunting with people you can relate to and enjoy. After all, enjoyment of your time in the outdoors is what it's all about.

CHAPTER 10

HUNTING THE ISLANDS

One of the most enjoyable hog hunting adventures awaiting sportsmen in California is a trip to one of the islands found off the southern California coast. While there are several islands nearby-- Anacapa, San Miguel, Santa Rosa, Santa Cruz, and Catalina, only the latter three offer any sort of hog hunting.

Santa Rosa Island is of the least interest to those who like to hunt hogs, simply because while the pig population is very large, hog hunting is only done in conjunction with very expensive hunts for the Roosevelt elk and mule deer that inhabit the island. Estimates by the National Park Service put the overall hog population on the island at around 1500. The hunting is conducted on the Vail & Vickers Ranch, and run by Wayne Long, head of Multiple Use Managers, P.O. Box 1210, West Point, CA 95255; phone (209) 293-7087. At this point there are no plans to hold hunts for hog hunting only on this island, according to Long.

However, Multiple Use Managers obtained the hunting rights to the Nature Conservancy's portion of Santa Cruz Island beginning with the 1989-90 hunting season, and Long has set up a quality hog hunting program here. This is on the northwest side of Santa Cruz; the east end hunting program has been run by Island Adventures for many years. More about their program in a minute.

MUM's hunting program is on a portion of Santa Cruz that couldn't offer any more ideal hog habitat if they tried. The area covers nearly 50,000 acres, and Long, a wildlife biologist, estimates

Glassing for wild boar on a sheer cliff overlooking the brilliant Pacific Ocean is different experience from mainland hunting. Santa Catalina, Santa Cruz, and Santa Rosa islands all offer good hog hunting. (Photo by Craig Boddington)

that there are some 4000 hogs on this portion of the property. "We trapped 650 pigs in a 5000-acre patch without trying too awful hard," he told me. "The place is full of wild hogs." This big chunk of the island is full of steep, brush-choked canyons interspersed with some pines and eucalyptus trees and other assorted vegetation. There is no shortage of cover for hogs to hide in, one reason the population is so strong and the hunting so good. The bag limit reflects this. "We'll let a hunter on a two-day hunt take two hogs, and someone on a three-day hunt can take three hogs," Long said. "We expect our success rate to be right at 95 percent for meat hogs, and 50 percent for trophy boars with two-inches or more of tusk."

MUM will allow four rifle hunting parties at one time, with a maximum of three hunters per guide. For bowhunters, four hunters per guide maximum is allowed, with a maximum of four parties. Also, bowhunters receive a 15 percent discount on the hunt package price. For more information on this operation, see Appendix A.

On the other side of the island, Jaret Owens of Island Adven-

Craig Boddington took this nice meat hog on the east end of Santa Cruz Island, and soon discovered that island hunting is the same as on the mainland in one respect--you still have to pack them out to the truck. (Photo by Craig Boddington)

tures (907 Daly Rd., Ojai, CA 93023; phone (805) 646-2513) has been conducting hunting for many years. His portion of the island covers about 10 square miles, but the cover is much more open than that found on the other half of the island. That means that hog numbers are relatively low, one reason Jaret only permits the taking of what he terms a "mature boar;" that is, a boar that will weigh over 100 pounds on the hoof and has some exposed tusk. "We don't shoot meat hogs," Owens said.

Most hog hunting here is done in conjunction with a hunt for Ramboullet sheep. It's a great deal for hunters, too, with a limit of one mature ram, two "meat" lambs, and one wild boar permitted per hunter over a two-day hunt. Owens offers something for everyone, with guided and non-guided hunts, and special hunts for archers, black powder shooters, handgunners, and riflemen. His $475 fee includes the two-day hunt, as well as charter air service to and from the island. Again, for more information, see Appendix A.

Santa Cruz has become very, very popular with bowhunters in

As of the 1989-90 season, Santa Catalina Island only permits archery hunting for wild boar and deer. Catalina has been a favorite of bowhunters for years, and offers some very good pig hunting at a reasonable price.

recent years. That's because the game is plentiful, the cost reasonable, and the shooting opportunities in one weekend can outnumber all the chances even a skilled archer may get on a week-long deer or elk hunt out of state that costs many times the money.

Catalina Island was, for many years, one of the more popular hunting destinations for southern Californians after deer, quail, and wild boar. In seasons past virtually any weapons were permitted, but that all changed in 1989-90, when the island changed its policy. Now only bowhunting is allowed anywhere on the island.

This beautiful island holds a good hog population, and hunting can be very good. Approximately 42,000 acres are open for hunting, with archers confined to camping in one of two designated camp areas. Each area has space for a maximum of 30 hunters. All hunts are non-guided now, so archers should bring pack frames and all the equipment necessary to butcher their game in the field and haul it back to camp, as well as an ice chest to keep it cool in warm weather. The price is certainly right, with the 1989-90 fee for a three-day hunt

Santa Cruz Island is like two different worlds. The west end is wide open, but the east end is thick and brushy, offering the best hog hunting by far. Sheep hunting is better on the east end. (Photo by Craig Boddington)

being $295, which includes transportation to and from the island.

Catalina is an island of varying habitat, with the hogs often spotted rooting on semi-open hillsides or down in deep, brushy canyons. The program is administered by Catalina Island Hunting Programs, P.O. Box 5044, Two Harbors, CA 90704 (no telephone number was available at press time). More information about the program can be found in Appendix A.

Hunting the islands for wild boar is quite an adventure. There's the sound of the surf crashing at night, the smell of the salty ocean, a cool breeze--and lots of game. Camps on Santa Cruz and, if you go there, Santa Rosa, are very nice indeed, with food to match and quality hunt operators. At Catalina there's always a trip into Avalon for an exquisite seafood dinner overlooking the beautiful harbor, as well as the city's entertaining and varied nightlife.

As they say in that TV ad, "Try it--you'll like it!" I haven't met anyone yet who didn't enjoy their island hunting adventure. I doubt you'll cast the first negative vote.

CHAPTER 11

GUNS & LOADS

I remember vividly my first wild boar hunt. It was a cool, overcast fall day nearly 15 years ago, while I was Managing Editor at <u>Western Outdoor News</u>. I'd been invited to hunt the Dye Creek Preserve near Red Bluff by then-manager Mike Ballew. Mike had also invited Gary Voet, the outdoor writer for the <u>Sacramento Bee</u> and an old college roommate and ball-playing buddy. Gary had never been big-game hunting before.

To make a long story short, the hunting was as it always is at Dye Creek -- lots of pigs scattered about the massive ranch. We hiked around awhile, and finally found a group of good-looking meat sows. I was up, and Mike and I crawled within a hundred yards or so of the herd. I took a prone position, rested the rifle on my day pack, settled the crosshairs behind the shoulder of the hog Mike pointed out, and squeezed the trigger.

At the shot there were hogs running everywhere, mostly over a little hill and out of sight. We sprinted over, and there, not 25 yards down the hill, lay my sow. The 100-grain factory Remington Core-Lokt bullet from my Browning BBR in .25-06 had taken out the heart, and the 150-pound sow was stone dead.

"Why, shoot, there's nothing to killing these pigs," I remember thinking rather smugly. "They're just like deer." Gary had shot a 200-pound boar with 2 1/2-inch teeth with my rifle earlier that morning, with identical results.

Since that day I've seen well over 500 wild hogs shot in the field.

I've seen them taken at ranges as far as an honest 400 yards, and as close as half a foot. I've seen all different types of rifle actions and calibers, bullet weights and designs, and factory ammunition and handloads used. I've seen them taken with handguns, both revolvers and bolt-action single-shots, shotguns using slugs, muzzleloaders, and archery gear.

All this hog hunting has changed my opinion of how easy these animals are to harvest. Wild hogs, and especially the larger animals weighing over 200 pounds on the hoof, are anything but easy to kill cleanly. Use the wrong bullet, a caliber that's too small, a broadhead that's not razor-sharp, and you're asking for problems. In this chapter we'll talk about the proper weapons to use for wild boar hunting. In Chapter 11, we'll discuss how to make the shot count.

Centerfire Rifles

As is the case with all big game hunting, the majority of sportsmen select a centerfire rifle as their weapon of choice. Modern big-game rifles are certainly our most efficient tools, allowing the hunter to take game cleanly at long ranges. But just as a painter has several different types of brushes to choose from to do a specific job, so does the rifle hunter have several different action types and calibers to select from. Choosing the right tool for the job only makes accomplishing the task that much easier. Conversely, the wrong tool will only make the job that much more difficult.

Most big-game hunters already own a centerfire rifle designed with deer hunting in mind, and this is what they take hog hunting. If you're a hunter who only owns one rifle and it's chambered for a popular deer cartridge, by all means use it. But if you're a serious hog hunter, you may want to consider buying a second rifle designed specifically for the type of pig hunting you do the most.

Rifle Actions

There are five basic rifle action types on today's market: bolt action, pump action, semi-automatic, lever action, and single-shot. In hog hunting any of the five will get the job done.

Most wild boar hunters use the same bolt action rifles they use for deer hunting with satisfactory results. Chris Dorsey's nice boar was taken with a .30-06 and 180-grain bullets.

Bolt Action rifles are far and away the most popular in the country, as they well should be. The actions are the strongest and most accurate of the repeating types, all the major manufacturers offer bolt guns, and the caliber selection is all-encompassing. I do 90 percent of all my rifle hunting with a bolt action rifle.

Bolt actions are excellent hog rifles. They offer relatively quick additional shots if needed, and nearly everyone owns one. They are also very accurate, allowing precision shot placement when those long, cross-canyon shots present themselves.

Pump Action rifles aren't nearly as popular here in the West as they are in the East, where whitetail hunting is done in thick woods and average shots are 75 yards or less. Pump guns give moderate accuracy, compared to bolt actions, but they are still accurate enough for shooting to 250 yards or so in the proper caliber.

For hog hunting, pump guns are excellent choices. Most have short barrels and swing quickly, even in tight cover. They make excellent brush guns, and are very handy when jumping hogs from

Pump action rifles aren't very popular in the West, but for thick brush and close cover situations, their fast follow-up shot capability can be a big advantage. Here Durwood Hollis is carrying a Remington pump in .308 Win.

their beds in thick manzanita and sage brush thickets. They're also lightweight, and easy to carry all day long.

Semi-automatic rifles have their following, and this action type has its merits. I once owned a Browning BAR in 7mm Remington Magnum that produced two-inch groups at 100 yards, plenty of accuracy for big-game hunting.

Semi-autos are good choices for hog hunting, too, especially in thick cover where quick second shots might mean the difference between pork in the freezer and nothing. However, semi-auto actions are a sonofagun to handload for, and they have been known to jam when they get dirty or muddy.

Lever action rifles make good hog guns, too, although proper caliber selection is very important. Their short barrels and relatively light weight make them a joy to carry all day, and as a brush gun they're hard to beat. Accuracy is moderate, but adequate out to medium ranges (under 200 yards).

One factor in favor of a lever action as a brush gun is its reliability. I've used quite a few different ones from companies like

Large-bore lever actions make excellent hog rifles. Their short overall length makes them easy to maneuver through heavy brush, and their actions rarely jam. This is a Marlin in .444.

Browning, Marlin, Winchester, and Savage, and never had a jamming problem, even in the worst dust, mud and rain imaginable. Today one of my favorite hog rifles is a Browning BLR in .358 Winchester.

<u>Single-shot</u> rifles are accurate, reliable, and chambered for some excellent long-range cartridges. For hog hunting, though, I don't recommend them for the simple fact that, unless you're really skilled with one, getting off a quick second shot is impossible. And without that additional shot, they are virtually useless as a brush gun. If you own a single-shot and want to take it hog hunting, don't be afraid to do so. Just make sure that you can place that first shot where you want it.

Calibers and Bullets

If you want to start an argument at a party, discuss politics, religion, sex -- or rifle calibers. Everyone who has hunted two times

The scoped single-shot specialty pistols are handy spot-and-stalk tools, though a steady rest is needed to fire them accurately. This Thompson Contender in .35 Remington took this big sow at 200 yards. (Photo by Durwood Hollis)

in their life is a ballistics expert, it seems, and everyone has definite opinions of what really "knocks 'em off their feet" every time.

In reality, the spectrum of rifle cartridges and bullets that will do the job on wild boar is so vast it's hard to decide where to begin. Under ideal conditions (an average-sized pig standing broadside a hundred yards away with the shooter having a good, solid rest) small calibers like the .223 will work -- if you place the bullet properly (in the head, in this case). However, ideal conditions rarely occur in the field, and I like to assume that they never will. When I go hunting, I try and match my rifle and cartridge to a worst-case scenario. That way, if that broadside shot does present itself I know I can make it. But, if the only shot I have is one quartering away in brush, I want to make sure that my rifle and cartridge combination are up to the task.

At this point I'll make a blanket statement and stick my neck out: The minimum I like to see hog hunters head afield with is a .270 using

Muzzleloading for wild boar is just plain fun, and these weapons will do the job out to 100 yards or so. I shot this 175-sow at 35 yards with a Thompson/Center Renegade in .54 caliber after jumping her from a bed.

150-grain pointed soft-point bullets. I have seen numerous pigs hit, and lost, when shot with small calibers like the .243, .25-06, .257 Roberts, .30-30 Winchester, and others. Hogs hit right behind the shoulder with a .270 using 130-grain bullets were lost when the bullet struck the elbow and came apart, with no penetration whatsoever.

On the other end of the spectrum, I've seen hogs hit at under 100 yards with a .375 H&H Magnum and 270-grain soft-points and lost. This has been the case with other heavy rifle calibers, too, though rarely.

I've come to believe that the best hog medicine, day in and day out, under a wide variety of conditions, are the medium big-game cartridges that use medium-weight bullets pushed at a fast, but not ultra-fast, velocity. Why? Because wild hogs are short yet stocky animals with a very thin skin and heavy bones. As we discussed in Chapter 3, large males have a thick cartilaginous sheath under the front shoulders. This sheath is so thick I once saw it stop a 240-grain jacketed hollow-point bullet from a .44 magnum revolver at 60 yards cold -- the hog had to be dispatched with a rifle.

The ultra-fast cartridges will often punch right on through a broadside pig without allowing proper bullet expansion, unless shots are taken at longer ranges. The medium-speed cartridges, on the other hand, allow proper bullet expansion and help ensure a quick, humane kill. The bigger rounds, like the .375 H&H, are designed for the largest animals on earth. Again, the bullet often passes right on through the hog without opening up.

Wild hogs, because of the fat around their bodies, also don't leave much of a blood trail when hit, making it difficult to track them if necessary. For that reason, I prefer .30 to .35 caliber cartridges for most of my hog hunting.

However, as I said at the beginning of this chapter, I've seen hogs taken with everything under the sun. I've shot them with cartridges like the .243, 6mm Remington, .25-06, .257 Roberts, .270, .280, 7mm Remington Magnum, .30-06, .307 Winchester, .308, .300 Winchester Magnum, 8mm Remington Magnum, .338 Winchester Magnum, .348, .358, .35 Whelan, .35 Remington, .444 Marlin, .375 H&H Magnum, and even a .416 Rigby. I've used all the Weatherby cartridges from .257 through .340, too. All have provided one-shot kills, so if you own a rifle chambered for any of these cartridges, take it hog hunting with confidence.

Bullet selection is also critical in hunting hogs. When using a cartridge with several choices, like the .30-06, go with the mid-range bullet weights in a spire-point design. This bullet design will afford maximum penetration even if you're shooting at the south end of a northbound hog, provide optimum accuracy and energy retention at the longer ranges, yet won't tear up a lot of meat.

Scopes vs. Open Sights

Most of us who own centerfire rifles have them scoped, and for 99 percent of all wild boar hunting your rifle should be scoped. There are very few of us who have shot enough with open sights in our lifetimes to be very good with them, especially out past the 100-yard marker. Another reason I don't like open sights is that most wild hogs are a dark color, and so are open sights. Trying to rest the bead properly in the notch of the rear sights against a background of grayish-black boar is tough to do. On my open-sighted .444 Marlin,

When using muzzleloaders, I prefer conical bullets to round ball because of their better overall penetration. This perfectly-mushroomed .54 caliber Buffalo Bullet was recovered from the off-shoulder of a big sow shot at 50 yards.

I've painted the front bead fluorescent orange, and this helps solve that problem.

For thick, thick brush work open sights are excellent. At any other time, a scope is the superior sighting tool.

I like scopes with a large objective lens, one that gathers the maximum light at dawn and dusk -- the best time to be hunting wild boar. Most of my scopes now have at least a 40mm objective lens, at that gives me that little extra edge during the gray light period.

The argument over whether the fixed power scopes are superior to the variables continues to rage on, but in my mind it was answered a long time ago -- the variables are the only way to go. Their versatility makes them the choice of serious hunters, and variable scopes made by name manufacturers are top-quality products that can stand years of the toughest field use -- and abuse. For most all my big-game hunting today I use 2-7X variables, but 1.5-5X and 3-9X variables are also excellent, provided they have the larger objective lens. If you choose a fixed power, 4X is still the best choice for the hog hunter.

Handguns for Hogs

Handgun hunting is gaining in popularity all across America. Hunting with handguns is certainly fun, but there are limitations. Know them, and you'll be well on your way to enjoying a hog hunt with your favorite pistol.

For the revolver hunter, there really are few choices that are adequate for hunting wild hogs. If you own a .357 Magnum and are thinking of bringing it pig hunting, do everyone a favor and don't. The .357 is a marginal deer cartridge, and shouldn't be considered for hunting wild boar under any but the most ideal conditions. The three revolver rounds recommended by most hog guides I know are the .41 Magnum, .44 Magnum, and .454 Casull. The heavy-jacketed hollow point bullets work well in all three, but I've found that the handloader who uses cast silhouette-type bullets will get deeper penetration and can extend his range a bit. But by and large, the revolvers are 75 yard and under weapons when it comes to hog hunting. When I hunt with a revolver, I prefer to get under 50 yards.

The scoped, single-shot specialty pistols are another story. Several of my good friends are well-known fanatics when it comes to these guns. They have proven to me that these are ultra-accurate, long-range weapons that are more than adequate for all North American big game -- if the proper caliber is selected.

And for wild boar that means one of the wildcat rounds. These include the 7mm Bench Rest Remington, 7mm T/CU, .30 Herrett, .357 Herrett, .300 Herrett, .35 Remington, .358 JDJ, .375 JDJ, and the like. All these cartridges, and others similar, will take wild boar cleanly, and do so at ranges that might surprise you. With a solid rest and a standing hog, I wouldn't hesitate to try a 250-yard shot with one of these pistol and cartridge combinations.

There are disadvantages, however. These scoped pistols must be shot from a rock-solid rest, which makes them a good choice for the spot-and-stalk hunter but useless for jumping hogs from the brush. Also, their quick second-shot capability is virtually nil. But if you own one and want to take it pig hunting, by all means go ahead. Just understand the limitations involved, stay within them, and you'll be sure of success.

Part of the fun in hunting wild boar is the chance to use weapons you enjoy shooting. Payton Miller used his favorite Thompson Contender in .30 Herrett to take this 225-pound sow right in its bed. (Photo by Durwood Hollis)

Shotguns and Slugs

Not many California hunters are familiar with the use of shotgun slugs for big game. In many parts of the country, notably the East coast and some parts of the upper Midwest, no rifles are allowed for deer hunting, but shotguns and slugs are. And believe me, in the right hands they are deadly weapons.

Serious slug hunters have special barrels designed specifically for slug hunting installed on their shotguns. These slug barrels come equipped with open sights, although the serious mount scopes on their shotguns. Slug barrels are rifled, standard shotguns true smooth-bores, and the accuracy difference is astonishing at the 100-yard mark. Yet shooting slugs from your standard shotgun barrel can be accurate enough to do the job for you, too.

If you're going to go hog hunting with shotguns and slugs, keep it to 12 gauge shotguns only. The 20 gauge slugs might take a deer, but a big boar would more than likely laugh at them. I have seen 12 gauge rifled slugs knock a 200-pound boar right off its feet at 50 yards, the slug passing right on through the animal. Durwood Hollis shot a good-sized sow once with a 12 gauge slug as the animal was heading right for him at 50 yards, and the results were spectacular. They are very, very effective.

The key to slug hunting is to keep the range to 75 yards and under, unless you have a souped-up slug gun you shoot a lot -- then the range can be doubled. Investing in a slug barrel for your shotgun would be a good idea, too. There are several good-quality slugs on today's market, including those produced by Federal and Remington, but the best I've ever seen are the BRI slugs. They are fast, accurate, and penetrate well.

Muzzleloaders

I've been a closet fan of muzzleloading rifles for quite a few years now. Originally I got into them to take advantage of several of the special big-game seasons other states offer, and I've never regretted it. I've shot elk in Colorado, deer in Utah, Colorado, and Montana, and pronghorn in Wyoming with muzzleloading rifles, and really enjoyed the experience.

I shot my first wild hog with my muzzleloader almost 10 years ago, and have since taken 15 others with these weapons. Hunting with a muzzleloader is quite a challenge. You have to stalk in as close as you can, trying to close the range to under 100 yards if possible. You have to make the first shot count, because no matter how fast you can reload that old front-stuffer, it isn't fast enough if you miss the first time. Hunting with these weapons takes a fair amount of skill, and there's little margin for error.

For wild boar, I don't recommend anything smaller than .50 caliber. I personally use a .54 caliber Thomspon/Center Renegade and .50 caliber Hatfield for all my muzzleloader hunting now, and both work like a charm. A .58 caliber rifle would also be a good choice for wild hogs.

I almost always use conical bullets when hunting wild boar with a muzzleloader, using a round ball only when I know I can stalk in very, very close and precisely place the shot. Conical bullets really

If you can stalk in close and make a precise shot, archery tackle will cleanly take even the largest wild hogs. Use a bow with a minimum peak draw weight of 50 pounds.

pack a wallop downrange, penetrate the fat and gristle of a wild hog very nicely, and help ensure a clean, quick kill. Cast bullets are good, but I like the pre-lubed Buffalo Bullets as well as any I've ever used. Round balls, on the other hand, have much less retained energy than the conicals, penetrate much less, and are generally less efficient on tough game like hogs.

Bowhunting

If you want to hear an experienced hog guide cry, call him and tell him you want to come hunting on his place with a bow and arrow. There isn't one around who doesn't have horror stories of missed shots, pigs hit and lost, and more goof-ups than you can imagine.

Most of these problems occur simply because the hunter in question is an inexperienced bowhunter who can't stalk, for one thing, and can't place his arrow accurately, for another. In the hands of an experienced hunter, however, archery tackle is quite deadly.

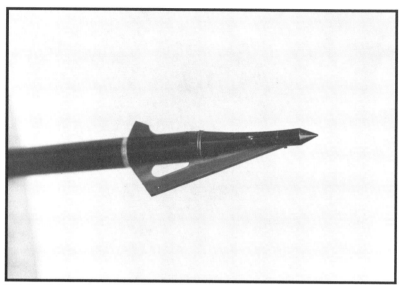

This fragile broadhead was destroyed by the front leg bone of an average-size sow. For best results when bowhunting, use broadheads with heavy blades and a cutting edge that extends right to the tip.

The foregoing is included to try and emphasize a most important point -- if you're going to hunt with bow and arrow, for heaven's sake practice, practice, practice before you come hunting. Make sure you can estimate ranges accurately (or use a range finder), have razor-sharp broadheads, and bring along the patience to stalk in close and let the pig position itself properly before you shoot.

Your bow should have a minimum draw weight of 50 pounds when hunting wild boar, and a 60-pound draw is better. Broadheads should be three- or four-bladed, and I've always preferred the type that has a cutting edge clear to the tip instead of the chisel point design. Tests show that the most important factor in arrow penetration on game is not the peak draw weight of the bow, which controls arrow speed, but the cutting ability of the broadhead itself. Chisel-point broadheads are fine for thin-skinned game like deer, but for tough animals like hogs, those that carry a razor-sharp cutting edge all the way to the point are much better.

When hunting with archery tackle, the best shot is one with the hog either perfectly broadside to you or slightly quartering away.

On public land, this may be the only end of a hog you'll see. For that reason, it's best to select an accurate rifle chambered for a cartridge that will penetrate deeply.

This is especially true for the largest boars, those tough guys with that thick sheath under the front shoulder. By letting the animal quarter slightly away, you can slip your arrow in behind the sheath and still angle it forward into the lungs.

Wild boar are excellent beginner's animals for bowhunters because of their poor eyesight. Get the wind right, and you should be able to sneak in very, very close to them. However, hit them wrong with an arrow and you've probably lost them, for as we mentioned before, they leave hardly any blood trail and are difficult to track. For that reason, take your time and stalk in as close as possible before shooting. Use a commercial range finder, if you have the time, to make sure you know the exact yardage to the target. When hunting from a stand, place yardage markers out in front.

But make no mistake about it -- a bow and arrow is a deadly combination in the hands of a skilled hunter. Hit a hog correctly with the arrow, and you can be sure you'll be feasting on a succulent ham dinner on Sunday.

The most important factor in selecting any weapon for hunting is to use one you're both comfortable and familiar with. In so doing you'll help ensure both an enjoyable hunt and a quick, clean kill. Also, choose a weapon suitable for the country you'll be hunting. For example, the only practical weapons for the majority of public land hunting are centerfire rifles and single-shot, long-range handguns; the chances are just too few and far between to risk blowing a rare opportunity with weapons that require you to close the range. An exception might be to carry a few shotgun slugs on a quail hunt, "just in case."

But again, the whole point is enjoyment. Maybe that's why I still carry my bow on public land.

CHAPTER 12

MAKE THE SHOT

It doesn't really matter what big-game species you're hunting, or what weapon you've selected, if you can't make the shot. Placement of the bullet, arrow, or slug is the most critical portion of any hunt. Place the projectile properly, and the result is a clean, quick, humane kill, the only kind that real hunters and sportsmen are satisfied with.

Your quarry deserves this respect from you. That means that before ever heading afield you have taken the time to become familiar with your weapon, and have practiced enough to make the first shot count. It also means that you don't take "Hail Mary" shots at running game, or any shot that you are not confident of making cleanly. And, if the worst happens and you do wound an animal, you take the time necessary to try and find it and finish the job.

Bullet Placement

When hunting wild hogs, you'll be hunting basically two types of animals--meat sows and boars, and trophy-class boars. Shot placement on both is basically the same. However, when hunting an animal primarily for the freezer, I try and make sure that I move into such a position that I can place my shot without ruining any edible meat at all. When hunting a trophy boar, it's a bit different. These are usually old, tough animals that will be ground into sausage; if I break his shoulder and blood-shot part of it that will eventually have to be discarded, I'm not too concerned.

Shot placement is the name of the game in any big-game hunting, and that means lots of practice before the hunting trip begins. Become so familiar with your weapon that using it becomes second nature.

Perhaps another look at Chapter 2 is in order now. Wild boar are built basically the same as deer, with hearts set low in the chest and large lungs set between the shoulders. In older, mature boars the cartilaginous sheath protecting the front shoulders can be a formidable obstacle, and anytime you're hunting these tough old animals you can't forget about that armoring. The heart is also set a bit farther forward in the chest than that of a deer, as is the diaphragm separating the heart/lung cavity from the digestive tract. Therefore, a wild hog hit a little too far back from the "sweet spot" just behind the shoulder will be gut shot, and you'll have big problems. Aim a few inches farther forward than on a deer and you'll be in good shape.

In hog hunting, the first rule of thumb is don't shoot at the southbound end of a northbound hog if you can avoid it. There are two reasons for this. First, the chances are good you'll hit--and ruin-- a ham, a cardinal sin. Second, you'll rarely ever shoot a hog that hasn't been feeding and/or at water. That means that his massive system of stomach and intestines will be full of partially-digested

Shooting at the southbound end of a northbound hog is never a good idea, but here, with the animal quartering away, the bullet can be aimed at the off-shoulder. This is a good angle on a big boar with heavy sheath under both front shoulders.

goo. This spongy mess will prevent all but the heavier caliber center-fire rifle and pistol bullets from penetrating it cleanly to the vitals, resulting in a wounded animal. Also, wild hogs that are eating well have lots of fat on them, another of Mother Nature's special paddings. This fat is thickest in the hips (I've seen as much as four inches of fat on a large sow's hips) and is very tough to penetrate.

If you get slightly above a hog moving at this angle and decide you just have to shoot, try placing the bullet right between the shoulder blades, where the neck meets the spinal column. Hit bone, and you've got a dead hog. However, stay alert. I once hit a meat sow with my .25-06 and 120-grain bullets at 50 yards exactly like this, and knocked her right off her feet. Seconds later she was up and running, heading for thigh-high barley and freedom. If I hadn't been on my toes and given her another round behind the shoulder she would have certainly gotten away for good. The first bullet had passed harmlessly through the neck muscle, hitting only meat and no bone or windpipe.

My own personal rule of thumb is to take a rest before shooting, unless the animal is point-blank and the cover too heavy. A pack frame can serve as a bench-rest solid shooting platform if no natural rest is available.

The classic shot, of course, is at a broadside animal. When hunting the better private ranches up and down the state, you really should see enough hogs that taking this kind of shot should not be a problem, even if you have to pass up an animal or two. On public land you take what you can get. You have to judge the situation and decide when it's time to shoot, and when it's time to wait.

The "pocket" right behind the front shoulder is the classic spot to pick when hunting any big-game animal that's broadside to you, and wild hogs are no exception. Place the bullet there and you'll be destroying heart and/or lung tissue, and though the animal may run a ways, it's yours. If you see a hog kick like a mule after placing the bullet in the pocket, you've probably hit the heart. One that gallops off full speed and shows little reaction has more than likely been hit in the lungs.

If the animal is quartering a bit to or away from you, the secret is to aim for the off-shoulder -- the shoulder you can't see. Visualize this spot on the animal and place the bullet to hit him there. If you do,

Bowhunters should strive to get as close as possible and allow the hog to turn broadside or quarter slightly away. This is not difficult to do if you keep the wind in your face and make no sudden movements. (Photo by Durwood Hollis)

you'll again be taking out heart and lungs, and that's just what you want.

Because I hunt wild hogs in brushy country frequently, and because of their tenacity for life, I don't want them running at all after they're hit. For that reason, I shoot the vast majority of my hogs now in the head, if I possibly can. This is a tougher shot to make than you might at first imagine, for the brain is small. If the animal is broadside, aim right for the base of the ear. Facing you, right between the eyes will do it. Bullet placement is critical on head shots, and I don't recommend them unless you're closer than 100 yards and have a rock-solid rest. But they don't ruin an ounce of meat, and when properly executed, you've got an animal that never has to be tracked.

Archers need to be a bit more careful, especially when hunting big boars. On these larger hogs, the ideal shot is either perfectly broadside, with the arrow placed right in the pocket, or with the animal quartering slightly away from the shooter. Then, the arrow can be slipped behind the cartilaginous sheath and angled forward into the lung area. Trying to punch an arrow clean through this heavy sheath is not a good idea. On smaller boars and meat sows, however, it poses no problem.

One lesson that's been learned the hard way over the years is to make sure the animal is dead--for good--before you start shaking hands and patting each other on the back. I remember vividly the time a bunch of us were at Dye Creek, field testing the then-new .356 cartridge. A big trophy boar was the target, standing still and broadside at 75 yards. The first shot turned him right over, all four feet sticking straight up in the air. The whooping and hollering started immediately -- and so did the boar. He was up and running at full speed, and it took eight more shots from the .356 and four from a .270 to finally stop him.

Admittedly, this is the worst case I've ever seen, but it emphasizes the tenacity a wild hog has for life. Hit them right the first time, and there isn't usually any problem. Hit them wrong, and you've got all sorts of trouble. With the .356 it was a case of poorly-constructed bullets blowing up on the hide, giving little penetration. Once you make the shot and the animal is down, keep it covered for a moment. Assume it is going to get up and run away. That way if the unforeseen does occur, you'll be ready.

Tracking Wounded Hogs

Wild hogs like brush -- the thicker the better. When they're wounded, even if it has occurred in open grain fields or grassy hillsides, rest assured they'll head for bedding areas. This thick cover is their security blanket, and once there they become very tough to find.

Tracking a wounded wild hog is not an easy task. The thick fat and loose skin works over a wound in a hurry, and the animals rarely leave a blood trail worth a darn. They are also usually with other hogs, in country that has been recently frequented by lots of other hogs. Picking up an individual track can be next to impossible under these conditions.

Unless you're hunting alone, it is always a good idea to have your

Be patient! Although Craig Boddington is only 50 yards from this herd of hogs, he has the wind in his favor and doesn't have to rush a shot. Craig waited until the black sow in the middle turned broadside; she never knew what happened.

partner act as a spotter, keeping his eyes glued to the animal after the shot. This will at least give you some idea at to where the hog is heading. If hit, it will begin to trail after the herd shortly, or take a slightly easier route around a hill or brush pile. If a vehicle is handy, have someone drive around and try to head them off at the pass while you try and track from the rear. Just remember that following up a wounded animal is often long, tedious work; patience and persistence will stand you in good stead now.

Always keep in mind that a wild hog is a tough, tough critter indeed. While good shot placement is always critical in any hunting, it is even more so on a tenacious animal like the wild boar. Just be sure to take your time, get a good rest whenever possible, and put the bullet or arrow right where you want it. That's the only way to achieve the results you want--a quick, clean, humane kill that wastes little meat.

CHAPTER 13

HOG GEAR

My friend Dwight Schuh and I spent 12 days humping it up, down, and all around the Weimenuche Wilderness Area of southern Colorado in August, 1988, bowhunting for what we would both consider big mule deer bucks. We traveled in weather that ranged from postcard-beautiful to freezing rain and wind. We hiked 10 to 15 miles a day, none on the level, at elevations exceeding 11,000 feet. We put in long, hard hours, and never did fling an arrow. And being outdoor writers, Dwight and I both carried hunting packs that weighed right at 20 pounds (we checked them on a spring scale we used to balance the packs on Dwight's two llamas).

I vividly remember one afternoon toward the end of the hunt. The skies had opened up, and the rain and hail was falling by the bucket. Dwight and I were both pretty beat up physically by this time, but our spirits still were as high as the peaks we were hunting. As we crawled under a big juniper bush to try and get out of the downpour, Dwight rubbed his shoulders, grinned that half-grin of his, and, as he tossed his pack to the ground, said, "Whatever happened to the days when we could just put a book of matches in our pockets and go hunting?"

That got us both to giggling like little kids at the circus. It also brought back flashes of hunts past, both when I was carrying way too much gear, and again when I wasn't carrying enough. There's a fine line between the essentials and just hauling along extra weight for no sane reason. Putting together a functional, no-nonsense hunting

The one item I never go back-country hunting without is my pack frame. I can carry a full weekend's gear and food in the bottom sack, and still have room to load a boned-out pig onto the exposed frame area.

pack takes some serious evaluation based upon field experience. Over the past 20 years I've come up with my list of gear, which is actually three lists, depending upon where I'm hunting, how long I'll be gone, and what the mode of transportation will be once the hunt begins. For example, I know I can get away with carrying lots of "luxury" items if I'm hunting with my vehicle as my base. Conversely, if I'm backpacking for a week, I know I have to shave it down to the bare essentials. A weekend pack frame hog hunt falls somewhere in between.

Which brings me to a very valid point in gear selection. Before you go into the sporting goods store and spend lots of your hard-earned cash on an impulse buy, purchasing something you'll probably never use, you have to realize that we hunters are really kids at heart. Admit it! When we go into the sporting goods store, we're like kids in a candy shop with money -- a very dangerous combination. We just can't resist all those shiny new toys. We all secretly believe

You can carry as much or as little ancillary gear into the field as you want, but after a few trips into the back country you'll leave all but the essentials behind.

that the kid who dies with the most toys wins, and if we buy something one of our buddies doesn't have, we're ahead in the race.

Fight the urge! Don't buy something unless it's part of your plan, the plan you've made and stuck with over the years about what gear works best for you. There's no need to own equipment that will collect dust in your garage for years, until the wife makes you get rid of it at the next garage sale. If you take the time to plan smart, you'll not only save money in the long run--why not buy a guided hunt instead?--and be toting around only the weight that will come in handy in taking care of the business of finding hogs, shooting them, and getting the meat to the butcher still fresh as a daisy.

Let's look at what you <u>really</u> need to be a hog hunter.

Backcountry Hunts

Backcountry hunting for wild boar in California is tough, tough work, pure and simple. The consistently successful wear out their boots as they travel far off the beaten path in search of game. They're

A useful field-care item is a lightweight saw. With one you can easily split briskets and stubborn pelvis bones, aiding the carcass in cooling quickly and completely.

prepared to bone their meat out and carry it back over steep terrain. To that end, they pare their gear down to the essentials.

No matter where I go hunting, my pack--either a day pack or the sack on my pack frame--contains the following items: flashlight, spare bulb, spare batteries; topographic map and compass; butane lighter; knife; small polycarbide sharpener; basic first-aid kit; 50 feet of nylon parachute cord; blaze orange plastic flagging; saline solution and small contact lens case (I wear contact lenses); spare prescription eyeglasses; spare boot laces; toilet paper in sealed ziploc bag; small roll of cloth athletic tape; small notebook & pen; hunting license. I always wear a wrist watch.

If I might possibly bivouac out overnight, as on a weekend backcountry hog hunt, I'll add the following: small camera, film; high-energy foods; two one-quart water bottles, full; space blanket; cloth sack for packing boned meat; cheesecloth game sack, in case I have to hang the carcass and leave it for any length of time. A lightweight sleeping bag, pad, and tube tent comprise my shelter.

My basic hunting gear includes the following: my weapon; spare

Wire drags are one of the handiest tools a hog hunter can carry. They keep the task of dragging hogs short distances from becoming a back-breaking torture test.

ammunition (rifle or handgun cartridges in a nylon belt pouch, arrows in my bow quiver); 8X or 10X binoculars; Swiss army knife; basic bow tools, if bowhunting.

I use two types of packs. If I'm going to hunt an area where I might have to move an animal any more than a quarter mile up and over a steep hill, I'll have a pack frame available. It's much easier to pack the animal this way than to drag him. My hunting pack frames all have gear bags attached for all my essentials. If I'm hunting where I might drag the animal, or by some slim chance be able to drag it to the vehicle, I'll hunt with a teardrop-shaped day pack with outside pockets large enough to accommodate my water bottles.

No matter how far into the back country I've gone, in my vehicle I always have the following: 86- or 100-quart ice chest for hauling meat, with a 25-pound block of ice already inside; smaller ice chest with cold drinks and food; propane lantern, in case I have to work on meat after dark; complete first-aid kit; spare weapons parts and ammunition; sleeping bag, pad, pillow; old ground cloth; notebook and pen; compact gambrel and pulley system, for hoisting carcasses for ease of butchering; five-gallons of water; alarm clock; light coat or sweatshirt; clean set of "travel" clothes in small duffel bag, including an old towel. If it "just might," I throw in a lightweight rain suit.

Guided and Ranch Hunts

On a guided or ranch hunt, you can bring along everything but the kitchen sink, the hunt operator permitting, because you'll be hunting primarily from a vehicle or making short hikes not far from roads. On these hunts you can bring along that spare coat, extra rifle or bow, or other nonessential items that are nice to have and fun to play with, but not really necessary to get the job done. You can also leave lots of the self-contained items, like the gambrel hook set-up, at home, as the guides will have these tools. No need to double-up on something you might lose or break if it isn't needed. Be sure to bring your copy of the hunt agreement, the guide's telephone number and directions to where you're supposed to meet.

There are a few marginal items that are nice to have and not listed above that may come in handy every now and then. A solid wire drag is a terrific tool, and makes dragging a hog so much easier than a piece of rope or cord. A large set of crock-sticks, for really getting an edge on a knife, is nice in camp. Forty-gallon trash bags can always be used for something. A boning knife makes stripping a carcass a snap.

It should go without saying that you have already sighted in and practiced with your weapon, and know it as intimately--almost--as a lover. I try never to make the first hunting trip of the season without servicing my equipment. I look over my packs for rips and weak parts, replace old flashlight and camera batteries, Sno-Seal my boots and replace old insoles, sharpen knives and broadheads, patch those holes in the knees of my jeans. I want everything to be in A-1 shape before I step out the door and head into hog country, including my vehicle. My hunting time is too limited and too precious to have even a single trip ruined by a malfunction that could have been prevented with an evening or two of tender loving care on the couch watching a ball game.

I'm sure yours is, too.

CHAPTER 14

FIELD CARE

Wild game has been a staple in my diet ever since I can remember. Growing up in what was then the tiny, unincorporated town of Moorpark, dad always shot two bucks during the early deer season, and that meat took up the lion's share of mom's freezer space. Venison and dove and quail and rabbits and trout were not only delicious and good for you, they were also budget stretchers for a family of four squeaking by on a young fireman's salary.

Later, when I'd moved away to Sacramento to go to college, a friend's parents invited me over for a venison barbecue. I vividly remember the thought of such a feast really getting the juices flowing. I hadn't deer hunted seriously for a couple of years -- a lack of funds, a job, a heavy class load and playing three sports just not leaving time for it. I missed my venison.

The dinner was a disaster, the meat tough and stringy and a little on the "wild" side. Of course I ate it anyway; a college kid never turns down a free meal. It wasn't until the following year that I understood the problem. I saw the hunter kill a deer, clean it half-heartedly, not wash the carcass, then take the bloody, hair-impregnated animal to the butcher shop. He fully expected to get back cut-and-wrapped, melt-in-your-mouth meat that couldn't be beat.

I can still see my dad in the garage in Moorpark hard at work on two fat bucks he'd shot that morning. The carcasses were hanging by the antlers from the rafters, and he meticulously carved away any blood-shot meat. Then he took the garden hose and washed them

131

thoroughly, making sure not a single hair or clot of blood was left. He wrapped them in cheese cloth sacks to keep ever-present flies off, and the next morning, after they had glazed over nicely, took them to the local butcher to hang in his cooler for a week before processing. The result was meat more tender and flavorful than any beef.

That dad was a good teacher who had the right attitude about meat care was a blessing I didn't fully realize until that disastrous barbecue some 15 years later. But the moral of the story is a simple one. If you hunt and are successful, you have a moral obligation as a sportsman to take the time and do the work necessary to ensure that the meat will be cared for properly. Wasting game meat is unforgivable, whether it be leaving it in the field to rot or caring for it so poorly that the final product is not fit to eat.

Know Your Limitations

With wild boar, proper meat care is by far a more critical matter than even with venison. Pork is a delicate meat that spoils very quickly, especially in hot weather. A downed hog needs to be cared for immediately. That means carefully cleaning the carcass, then cooling the meat. Failure to do so can result in green, spoiled meat.

This point is much more important for the do-it-yourself hunter who decides to accept the challenge of a public land hunt and backpacks into a remote canyon. On a private ranch or a guided hunt, it's the guide's responsibility to initially care for the meat. Most of these hunts occur relatively close to a vehicle which makes meat care much easier. Getting the carcass to a meat shed, in an ice chest, or to the local butcher isn't a problem, so cooling the meat won't be critical. But in the back country, where you might be looking at a half-day's hike back to the car, you have to be much more careful.

I learned this lesson the hard way. A friend and I were hunting on public land in the central coast region, hiking two solid hours in the dark to be atop a specific ridge a little before daybreak. It was June, and the day promised to be a scorcher. As luck would have it, my friend shot a fat meat sow right off the bat out of a string of a dozen or so hogs. We field dressed the animal and hung it in the shade of a big oak tree, then sat down and talked it over. Should we

John Higley shot this prime sow on a hot summer's day. To ensure that the meat stayed fresh and flavorful, he dressed the hog quickly and had the entire carcass on ice in less than an hour.

pack this pig out now, or hang it in the breeze and hunt some more?

In the end we wrapped the carcass in cheese cloth and went looking for the rest of those hogs. We hunted until about noon, when the temperature was right at 100 degrees. We then decided we best head on back, both of us having home obligations the next day.

By the time we got back to the vehicle at about four o'clock, that pig had plain spoiled. The breeze never came up that day, but I doubt it would have made much difference. We took it to the meat locker anyway, hoping the butcher could at least save some sausage meat, but no luck. We had to discard 100 pounds of the best eating meat. That's the only time that has ever happened to me. I promised that come hell or high water, it never would again. I still feel terrible about the whole thing.

In the back country, the most important thing you can do after killing a hog is to field dress it, then get the meat cooled down. Failure to do so will result in a spoiled carcass, or at least one that doesn't taste quite the way it should.

This calls for some common sense. If the weather is summertime-hot, as it was for us, and you're a ways from the vehicle, get your animal on the pack frame and back to the ice chest right now. If it's wintertime-cool, you might be able to hang the cleaned carcass in a tree for awhile and hunt some more, but that's still taking a chance.

Don't hike back into a remote area farther than you can physically handle the work of getting a dead animal out. Most of us overestimate how tough we are, thinking we can hunt several miles of rough terrain easily. You may be able to hike in and cover some ground, but can you carry a boned-out carcass all the way back after 10 or more hard hours of hunting? One way to alleviate the problem is to hunt with a buddy with whom you've made an agreement to kill only one hog between you if you're more than a few miles back. That way you can each carry half the load out, then split the meat.

I have a friend who's getting up in years a little bit (he's a blip under 50 now) who still thinks he's tough as nails (he's still pretty good, but not nearly as good as he thinks). A few years ago he took his pack frame and hiked a few miles into some BLM country in mid-August to do a little deer hunting. As luck would have it, he killed not one but two bucks on a morning that reached 100 degrees well before noon. My friend also did not take any water with him, and by the time he had field dressed the deer he was seriously dehydrated. He covered the carcasses with grass and stumbled back to camp, where he drank a six-pack of soda pop, then slept for several hours. I thought we were going to have to rush him to a hospital, he was that spent. By the time he woke up and we got back to the deer (it was after dark) both had completely spoiled.

As an aside, my best hunting buddies and I have actually seen huge boars animals we estimated at near 300 pounds on the hoof, in a remote back country area near dark. On more than one occasion the conversation at that moment has gone something like this:

"Do you see that big black boar over there?!"

"What boar? I don't see any pigs. You must be hallucinating again."

"You're right. I must be losing it. I can't see anything, either."

We knew what shooting such a huge hog would mean--a hour-and-a-half of cleaning and boning, then three hours of steep, horrible, in-the-dark hiking to the truck with each of us struggling under near-100 pound packs. Sometimes it's just not worth it.

Know your limitations, and hunt within them.

Basic Field Dressing

Field dressing a wild hog isn't any different than field dressing a deer. It's a simple process, easily accomplished if you have the right tools. In this case that means a sharp hunting knife, a whetstone of some kind, and something to put the carcass in. Here's what you need.

* Sharp hunting knife, with blade length of anywhere from four to six inches best. Drop-point and clip-point designs are best.
* Small knife sharpener, either a whetstone or polycarbide sharpening tool.
* Gambrel hook and rope (for hanging carcass).
* Water (for washing both carcass and your hands).
* Old towels or rags (for drying both carcass and you).
* Large ice chest.

If you are hunting in the back country, you'll also need cheese-cloth-type game bags, for wrapping around the meat and keeping flies off as it initially cools down, and a cloth meat sack for loading the meat into and strapping it on the pack frame.

OK, you've finally done it! You've shot a wild boar, have all the tools, and are ready to begin the field-dressing process. Here's how to go about it efficiently and thoroughly.

Step 1: Make sure the animal is really dead! Seems obvious, but novice hunters often get so excited that they walk up to a downed animal they're sure is stone dead, only to have it get up and run off into the brush. Of course they've laid their weapons down, and a finishing shot is out of the question. Approach a wild boar cautiously from uphill and behind. If you can touch its eyeball with an object (stick, small rock, etc.) and it doesn't blink you can be sure the animal is dead. Now you're ready to begin.

Step 2: Turn the hog onto its back, with the head facing slightly uphill. Get behind the animal, grasp the two hind legs and spread them apart. If a friend can't help with this, use your knees and body to keep them spread open. Take the sharp knife and make a circular cut around the anus, cutting as deeply into the meat as you can.

Step 3: Now take the knife and make a small cut into the belly area, beginning in the area between the legs (right alongside the penis in a boar). You want to cut deeply enough to get through the skin and the fat directly underneath, but not so deeply that you cut into the organs. Taking care not to do this, cut from the beginning all the way up the belly forward to the base of the breast bone.

Step 4: Lay the knife aside and reach into the chest cavity and remove the stomach, intestines, and other organs that come away easily. Take care not to pop the bladder, which will usually be full of urine that can taint the meat. As the intestines come out (and there are several feet of them), you'll notice the large intestine is sort of stuck in the anal cavity. If your initial cut didn't loosen it sufficiently, you may have to work a bit to get it out. Do so now.

Step 5: Use the knife to cut away the diaphragm, the thin wall of muscle that keeps the heart and lungs separated from the lower intestinal tract. This will expose the heart and lungs, which must now be removed. You can do most of this without the knife, though it may be needed to cut through the wind pipe. Some hunters will first cut right through the sternum, making removal of the heart and lungs much easier. This is up to you.

Step 6: You're almost done. Now, lay the knife down and move to the front of the hog. Grab it by the front legs and lift it as high as you can, allowing the blood remaining in the chest cavity to drain out through the hole that used to house the anus.

Step 7: Now move to the back legs, and use the knife to make one incision in each leg. This cut must be made between the Achilles tendon (the thick tendon that, on humans, connects the heel of the foot with the back of the leg) and the leg bone. There's a thin patch of skin here to cut through, that's all. Take the gambrel hook and run one end through each of these cuts, then use the gambrel to hoist the animal up off the ground. You only need to elevate it so that the nose is slightly off the ground.

Step 8: You're ready to begin skinning the animal now. Start at the back legs, making a circular cut around the knees but taking care

A butcher can't turn out first-rate meat products for you if you give him a poorly cared-for carcass. Take the time to thoroughly clean your hog up, and you'll be rewarded with some of the best-tasting meat you've ever had.

not to cut the Achilles tendon. Next make a long cut down the back of each leg to its junction with the now-open chest cavity. Use the tip of the knife to carefully skin the legs and lower back, working down to the chest, the front legs, and finally the head. Skin the front legs as you did the rear, only working up from the ankles to the shoulders.

Step 9: The animal should now be skinned completely, except for the head. Since we're not saving the head for the taxidermist on this hog, we'll simply remove it. To do so, use the knife to cut the neck meat until the blade reaches the bone, then continue in a circular motion all the way around the neck. Once that's done, have a buddy hold the rear legs while you firmly grasp the head and twist it in a full circle. This will break the neck bone right where your knife cut the neck muscle, and it will drop right off.

Step 10: You now have a completely gutted and skinned carcass hanging before you. All that's left is the detail work. Take the knife and cut away any blood-shot meat. If the bullet happened to strike a large bone and come apart, don't be surprised if this is quite a bit. It

If you're hunting on a private ranch with a walk-in meat locker, check to see that its temperature is at or near the 38-degree mark. At this setting, your meat will stay fresh for days.

could be an entire shoulder. Blood-shot meat isn't any good, and the butcher will in fact cut it away himself after he's weighed the entire carcass and charged you for it anyway. Trim away large pieces of excess fat, but leave a little trim for the butcher to work with. Be sure to cut away any remaining pieces of organs and bone chips. After you're done, wash the carcass down thoroughly with the garden hose. An old wife's tale says to never wash wild meat with water, that it will taint the flavor of the meat. Hogwash! The best thing you can do is to completely hose the carcass down, washing away any blood and other undesirable residue. Make sure the carcass is in a cool, shady spot, and let it drip dry. If this is outside, wrap it in cheesecloth game bags to keep flies and bugs off. Make sure it's hanging in an area that is dust and dirt free. You want to give the butcher a spotlessly clean carcass to work with.

Step 11: Once the carcass is very clean and relatively dry, it's time to go to the butcher. If you can transport the carcass whole, great; do so. If not, get the largest ice chest you can find (86- and 100-quart

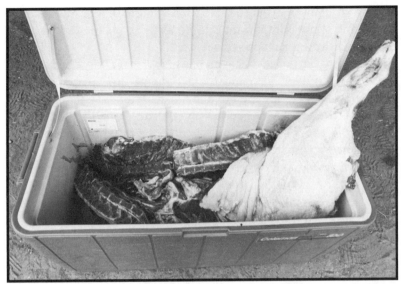

Never go hog hunting without an ice chest large enough to hold the amount of pork you expect to transport to the butcher. I always leave a chest with 25 lb. block of ice in my vehicle when back-country hunting "just in case."

chests are ideal) and quarter the animal. This means removing the front shoulders, backstraps, tenderloins, and back legs, laying each piece in the chest. Bone the ribcage out for sausage meat. Cover it all with ice, seal the chest tightly, and you're ready to go.

Backcountry Boning

If you're in the back country and miles from the truck, the answer is to bone the carcass out to eliminate any and all excess weight. Here's what I do when a packing chore is in order.

Follow all the above steps through Step 9. I then open my cloth game bag up, and get ready for boning. How you bone the animal will be largely dependent upon four factors: 1) How large is the animal?; 2) How far is it to the truck?; 3) How tough is the hike?; and 4) Do you have any help carrying the load out?

I figure that I can carry a maximum of 75 pounds comfortably out of a tough place, if the hike is only moderately steep and the distance under five miles. You may be able to carry more or less, but that isn't important. What is important is to honestly assess the task at hand, then bone the animal accordingly.

If the hog is small and I have some help, I may choose to not bone the front shoulders. Boning them reduces the meat to ground sausage, while keeping the bone in means I can have them smoked and cook them on the barbecue -- my favorite. But if I'm alone or the hog is a big one, I'll bite the bullet and bone the shoulders out.

Whatever you decide, begin the job at the front shoulders, since they're the closest to the ground. After I have the front shoulders taken care of, I bone off the back straps and carefully remove the tenderloins. Again, depending upon the size of the hog, the distance to the truck, and the amount of help I have, I may or may not bone out the rib cage and neck for ground sausage.

Last, but certainly not least, are those delicious hams. Boning the hams is easy, and won't affect how they're cooked at all. I like to first take each off the carcass, done by cutting the meat down to the ball-and-socket hip joint that holds everything on. Once the hams are off, I lay them on a clean ground cloth and make a circular cut around the hocks at the knee joint. Then make a straight incision from the hock to the ball joint, cutting all the way to the bone. You can then fillet the ham right off the leg bone. Cut the hock off at the knee joint (do it last, it makes a great handle when filleting), and presto! One boned out ham.

Once the hog is boned out, load the meat into a cloth meat sack and either drop it into the pack sack, or strap it securely to the frame. It's much easier to carry if the heavy part of the load is high on the frame. You're ready for a labor of love -- packing the boned carcass to the vehicle. When you get there, you'll hopefully have an ice chest large enough to hold all the meat, and a little ice to cover it up. On the way home stop and buy more ice. You can never use too much.

When caring for your hog, no matter where you are it's important to keep the meat as dirt-free as possible. It's amazing how easily dirt can impregnate itself into meat, forcing you (or the butcher) to cut it away. The Golden Rule of meat care is simple. Keep it clean, and cool it down. That's the only way to ensure that the final product will be fresh and flavorful at the table.

CHAPTER 15

THE SAVORY BOAR

Wild hogs have become California's number one big-game animal for several reasons. They're available over much of the state, and wherever they are introduced populations thrive. A season that never closes is another reason for their popularity. You can hunt wild hogs 365 days a year, giving sportsmen a challenging hunting opportunity when other game is protected.

But one of the big reasons the wild boar is so popular as a game animal is its sweet, succulent meat. People who don't particularly care for the taste of other wild game animals rarely complain when served a slice of wild boar ham, a rack of barbecued ribs from a fat meat sow, or a patty of spiced wild boar sausage to complement their breakfast eggs.

Those concerned with nutrition will be pleased with the composition of wild boar. Unlike domestic pork that is often injected with chemicals, laced with fat, high in cholesterol, and preserved with nitrites and other undesirable concoctions, wild boar is a healthy cut of meat. Obviously there are no preservatives in wild game, and the animals have grown big and strong in a natural manner, on foods provided by Mother Nature. The meat is extremely lean. The fat can be trimmed off easily, and there is rarely any marbling of fat in the muscle tissue itself. It is high in protein, vitamins, and minerals. I personally will not consume domestic pork in any form, but there's not a cut of wild boar I won't readily eat.

In Chapter 14 we detailed how to properly care for wild hogs in the field. This care cannot be overemphasized. Pork is a delicate meat, much more prone to spoilage than venison. It needs prompt attention once the animal is down to ensure that it will provide delicious meals unlike any other you'll ever have.

There are several ways to prepare wild boar. You can follow just about any recipe you use for domestic pork, and the results will be more than satisfactory. It is important to keep in mind that wild boar is a very lean meat, much more so than domestic pork, and care must therefore be taken to keep from drying the meat out by overcooking. How you have the meat butchered will also affect how you prepare it for the table. If you do the cutting and wrapping yourself, you can control the kinds and sizes of the cuts exactly. When you take it to your local butcher for processing, be sure to tell him just what you want done. In many instances you'll have the option of having the meat smoked or cured, a process I recommend highly. It's a rare wild hog that I bring home now that I don't have smoked entirely, save for the ground sausage. I also like to have specialty sausages and salamis made on occasion. Good butcher shops can make just about anything you want, including popular sausages like chorizo, moist and dry salamis, wine smoked sausage, and others. They can also control the amount of spicing they add to the meat, from mild to hotter than the proverbial pistol. You're limited only by your imagination.

Finding a good butcher shop that will do a first-rate job of processing, cutting, and wrapping wild boar can take some looking. Do your searching before the hunt so that your meat can be dropped off at a shop you have confidence in immediately. Most ranch operations can recommend a local butcher shop that they deal with regularly, and these are generally good people to use. It will pay to visit a few butcher shops close to your home with the intent of finding one that will do the kind of job you will be satisfied with. That way when you drive home with an ice chest full of meat you can drop it off immediately, satisfied that it will be taken care of properly.

Here, then, are several favorite ways to prepare wild boar, all guaranteed to please. Bon appetit!

On the Barbecue

The barbecue is as California as the beach and the Sierras. And the barbecue is a terrific place to prepare wild boar. I like to add a few hickory chips to the charcoal every now and then to give the meat a slight smoky flavor. The key to barbecuing wild boar is to not overcook it. Make sure the meat is done all the way through, yet not so done that it's dry. That's a delicate line to draw, so pay close attention to the cooking.

Barbecued Pork Chops

6 large chops with rib bones
1 1/2 cups barbecue sauce
garlic powder

peppermill-ground pepper
2 tbsp. butter or margarine
1 medium brown onion

Saute onions in butter on stove, and set aside. Place chops on the BBQ, and brush liberally with your favorite BBQ sauce. Sprinkle lightly with garlic powder and pepper. Turn, and repeat process (note: it's hard to use too much sauce). When done, remove, cover with grilled onions, and serve with additional sauce and onions on the side.

Barbecued Front Shoulders

1 whole smoked front shoulder
2 cloves garlic, cut into slivers

barbecue sauce

Cut small slits in shoulder, and insert garlic slivers. Place on BBQ and smother in your favorite BBQ sauce. Keep heat medium-low, and cook, turning and basting, until done (about an hour). If your BBQ has a top, keep it closed. This has been a favorite at several wild game feeds and parties I've had over the years. Slice thin slices from the shoulder, and serve.

Boar Burgers

1 lb. ground wild boar sausage, spiced
1 lb. ground venison
1 small brown onion, chopped

1 dozen onion rolls
A1 steak sauce, to taste
barbecue sauce, to taste

In a large mixing bowl, combine meat and onion. Make patties, place on BBQ, and pour on the A1 or barbecue sauce to taste. Turn, and add more A1. Serve on onion rolls, with your favorite garnishes.

Succulent Roasts

Wild Boar roasts make a fine main course, especially at holiday time. These recipies are designed to produce a roast that is both moist and tender, and full of flavor. One method I've used very successfully in the past, both for roasts and smaller hams, is to cook them overnight in a crock pot. By adding twice the liquid recommended for your crock pot, and cooking on slow heat for 10 to 12 hours for a five pound roast, the meat is about as tender as it gets. I like to add pineapple juice, apple juice, or a mixture of half water and half hearty burgundy wine as my crock pot liquid.

Beer-Braised Boar Roast

2 1/2 lb. boneless boar roast
2 cloves garlic, slivered
7 oz. beer
1 can (8 oz.) tomato sauce
1 tbsp. instant beef bouillon
2 large brown onions, skinned and quartered

6 slices fresh, lean bacon
3 tbsp. chopped fresh parsley
4 small potatoes, peeled and quartered
1/4 cup flour
salt, pepper to taste

Cut small slits in top of roast; insert garlic slivers. For marinade, combine beer, tomato sauce, bouillon in glass bowl. Add roast. Cover and refrigerate overnight, turning once. Line baking pan with aluminum foil. Place roast in pan; save marinade. Roll bacon in parsley; criss-cross atop roast. Bake in pre-heated, 450 degree oven 15 minutes, then remove. Set oven to 325 degrees. Add vegetables to roast. Dissolve flour in marinade, and pour over roast and vegetables. Sprinkle with salt and pepper. Cover with more foil, and bake 1 1/2 to 2 hours, or until meat thermometer registers 180 degrees.

Simple Pot Roast of Boar

boar shoulder roast	2 skinned brown onions, sliced
salted water to cover	2 carrots, peeled and sliced
2 cups water	1 cup diced celery
3 cups apple cider	1/2 tsp. dry sage

Simmer meat in salted water, covered, for 1 1/2 hours. Drain and return to pot with remaining ingredients. Cover and simmer until tender. Make gravy from cooking liquid. Slice thin and serve over hot, buttered egg noodles.

Pork Chops

Pork chops from a wild boar are about as delicious as it gets. Make sure the butcher leaves plenty of rib bone and meat attached when he cuts and wraps your hog. I like to have my chops smoked now, and these recipes will work well on both smoked and plain chops. See the "On The Barbecue" section at the beginning of this chapter for the best way to prepare chops on the BBQ. That's the way I like them best, but here is a delicious alternative.

Cranberry Chops

6 pork chops	2 oranges
2 tbsp. butter	1 lemon
salt, pepper to taste	1 lime
4 cups frozen or fresh cranberries	1 cup granulated sugar

Brown chops slowly in a skillet in butter, seasoning with salt and pepper. Place in a greased casserole dish, and cover chops with cranberry relish. Cover and bake at 350 degrees at least 1 1/2 hours, or until tender. To prepare cranberry relish, grind in blender the cranberries, oranges, lemon and lime; mix well, add sugar to taste - but don't make it too sweet.

Heavenly Ham

The most prized cut from any wild boar are the two hams. Hams should be cured or smoked by your butcher, in my opinion, to give them all the flavor they can have. Hams can be baked, of course, just as you would prepare a store-bought ham, and the results will be excellent. The crock pot is another good way to prepare a ham; just make sure to use plenty of liquid. Below are a couple of adventuresome ways to prepare your hams. They take some doing, but are well worth the effort.

Boned Ham Epicure

1 ham, cured or smoked	2 brown onions, skinned and chopped
1 1/2 quarts bread crumbs	1 tsp. crumbled sage
1/2 cup melted butter	1/4 tsp. rosemary
3 diced celery stalks	salt, pepper to taste

Melt butter in large skillet, then cook onion, celery until done without browning. Remove from heat, and add bread crumbs and seasonings. Toss lightly with fork to blend seasonings (add more to taste if desired). Add a bit of water if you prefer moisture stuffing. Set aside. With sharp knife remove bone from whole ham. Stuff bone cavity with sage & onion stuffing. Season ham with salt and pepper. Extra stuffing may be placed in pan, along with vegetables like carrots, potatoes, bell pepper, and celery. Roast at 350 degrees for 30 minutes per pound, basting with pan drippings. Allow to cool a bit before carving, then slice thin and serve.

Roast Hindquarter of Boar

1 hindquarter with bone, cured or plain
1/4 lb. butter, melted
1/2 cup chopped bell pepper
1 quart catsup
1 tbsp. salt
1 brown onion, chopped
2 garlic cloves, minced

2 cups tomato juice
2 cups hot water
2 tbsp. brown sugar
1 tbsp. hot pepper flakes
1 tbsp. ground black pepper

Soak hindquarter in heavy salt brine (1 lb. salt and 1 pint vinegar per two gallons water) for 24 hours; drain. Mix a marinade of all ingredients listed, and warm in kettle. Place hindquarter in large tub and pour marinade over it. Cover, and allow to marinade for two days in refrigerator, turning frequently. Remove from marinade and cook covered on medium heat on the barbecue for approximately 20 minutes per pound. Baste frequently with marinade. An average 10-14 lb. hindquarter should be done in four or five hours, and will feed 10 people.

All That Ground Meat

A wild boar will provide you with lots of ground meat. A front shoulder or ribs or other cuts of this type can be turned into ground meat. Ground boar results in two things -- unspiced ground meat, and spicy bulk sausage, assuming you don't have salamis made from it. The sausage is great cooked up as patties and served at any meal, not just breakfast. It's also a nice addition to meat loaf, chili, lasagna, as a pizza topping, and other casserole-type dishes. The plain ground meat is just that -- and with a little imagination and a judicious use of the spice rack, can be transformed into a world of delicious foods.

Spicy Ham Loaf

1 lb. fresh ground meat (I prefer venison)
1 lb. spicy bulk wild boar sausage
3/4 lb. ground smoked ham
3 eggs
1 1/2 cups milk
3 celery stalks, chopped

2 small cans chopped black olives
1 1/2 cups fine dry bread crumbs
6 tbsp. packed brown sugar
peppermill-grind black pepper
paprika, garlic powder, celery salt
1 medium carrot, chopped

Combine eggs and milk, add bread crumbs and spices to taste. Add celery, carrots, 1 can olives. Mix well with ground meats and pack firmly into greased loaf pans. Mix brown sugar with just enough water to form a thick paste. Spread on top of ham loaf, and top with remaining can of olives. Bake until done at 350 degrees (about one hour). Let cool 15 minutes before slicing. Or, bake ham loaf in greased muffin cups 45 minutes at 350 degrees, let cool for 10 minutes, then turn out onto broiled pineapple slices. This makes a delicious and attractive buffet supper.

Spicy Meatballs

4 lbs. spicy boar sausage
(or unspiced ground meat, if you prefer)   2 eggs, beaten
1/8 tsp. allspice   1/4 lb. butter
1/4 tsp. tabasco sauce   1/8 tsp. thyme
1/2 tbsp. ground pepper   3 cups cracker crumbs

Mix meat, cracker crumbs, melted butter, and eggs. Season with remaining ingredients. Then either fry softly in vegetable oil or butter, or bake at 350 degrees until done. These are the perfect addition to spaghetti sauce, or may be served on their own (try melting a little Swiss or jack cheese on them first).

Wild Boar Casserole

1 lb. spicy bulk sausage   1/4 tsp. garlic powder
1 lb. unspiced ground wild boar   1 7 oz. package elbow macaroni
1 cup chopped onion   1 cup dairy sour cream
1/4 tsp. ground pepper   2 tbsp. sherry (optional)
1 can condensed cream of mushroom soup   1 17 oz. can sweet peas, drained

Combine ground meats, onion, seasonings, shape into small meatballs, and brown in small amount of butter. Stir in soup, cover, and simmer 10 minutes. Remove from heat. Cook macaroni according to package directions. Stir sour cream, sherry, macaroni, and peas into meat mixture. Pour into 2 1/2 quart casserole dish; bake covered at 325 degrees 35 minutes.

Cabbage Leaves & Boar

1 large cabbage head, washed and drained   1 cup raw wild rice
1 1/2 lbs. spicy sausage or unspiced ground boar   2 tbsp. butter
3 large onions, peeled and chopped   1 tsp. dried mint leaves
3 beef bullion cubes, dissolved in 2 cups boiling water

Immerse cabbage head in boiling water for 5 minutes; drain and separate leaves. Reserve 12 outer leaves and put remaining leaves into large, well-greased pot with tight-fitting lid. Mix meat, onions, rice and place three heaping tablespoons on each reserved cabbage leaf, roll tightly, folding edges over and secure with toothpicks. Place on cabbage leaves in pot. Cover with bullion, adding water to cover completely. Dot with butter. Cover tightly; steam 1 hour.

The Ultimate Sloppy Joes

2 lbs. ground wild boar   2 cups tomato catsup
3 tbsp. vegetable oil   1/2 cup water
salt, pepper, garlic powder to taste   2 16-oz. cans red kidney beans, drained
1/4 lb. fresh mushrooms, sliced   8 onion rolls, halved

In large skillet, heat vegetable oil and stir in meat. Cook, stirring frequently, until meat looses its pinkness (don't overcook!). Drain meat in colander. Put back into skillet, and sprinkle with spices. Add catsup, mushrooms, water. Simmer gently for 30 minutes. Add kidney beans, heat thoroughly, and serve over warmed buns halves that have been buttered, sprinkled lightly with garlic powder, and toasted under broiler.

APPENDIX A: GUIDES & RANCH HUNTS

Just a few weeks before sending the first edition of "Hunting Wild Boar in California" to the printer, I mailed a survey out to 60 guides and ranches throughout California who reportedly cater to wild boar hunters. Two mailings were sent to give each guide ample opportunity to complete the single-page written survey and mail it back to me.

Out of those original 60 surveys, only 15 responded. Two had moved and left no forwarding address. Those surveys that were returned were reprinted in previous editions to give the reader an idea of what each guided hunt offers. In subsequent years, I learned that many wild boar guides go out of business, or change their business, fairly often. Yesterday's excellent operation is possibly tomorrow's mediocre service, or no longer in business. For that reason before this edition went to press, I resurveyed all the guides listed in previous editions, plus some new operations I've become aware of.

The following list is as up to date possible at press time. This appendix is offered as an information source only. In no way does it endorse any of the operations listed. It is very important that hunters contact each guide they are considering before booking a hunt to help ensure a quality hunting experience. Prices, of course, may have changed, and are presented to give the reader a general idea of what each hunt costs.

Name: **Bow & Bore Ranch, P.O. Box 2102, Livermore, CA 94551.**
Phone: Day (408) 897-3262; Evening (408) 897-3262.
Years As Hog Guide: Eight years.
Hunters Guided Per Year? 100.
Approximate Success Rate? Meat hog, 95%; Trophy Boar, 95%.
Maximum Number of Hunters/Trip?: Six (2 hunters/1 guide rifle; bow hunts unguided.).
General Hunting Area: 30 miles south of Livermore.
Hunts Conducted On: Private land only, approximately 1000 acres.
Months Hunting Available: All year.
Hunting Methods Used: Spot & stalk.
Weapons Allowed: Rifles; muzzleloaders; handguns; archery gear.
Guide Fees: Meat hog, $400 rifle, $350 bow; Trophy boar, $450 rifle, $350 bow.
Trophy Boar Criteria: Two-inch tusks.
Do Guide Fees Include:
    Field dressing of game? Yes
    Hunt transportation? Yes
    Food or drinks? No
Do You Also Offer:
    Place to sleep? Yes (no cost)
    Meat locker facilities? No
    Meals/drinks? No
    Camping in tents/trailers/RV's: Yes
    Transport of head to taxidermist? Yes
    Transport of meat to butcher? No

Name: **Jack Beguhl, 403 N. Suey Rd., Santa Maria, CA 93454.**
Phone: Day (805) 928-5376; Evening (805) 928-5376.
Years As Hog Guide? 13 years.
Hunters Guided Per Year? 80.
Approximate Success Rate? Meat hog, 75%; Trophy Boar, 25%.
Maximum Number of Hunters/Trip? Six, two hunters/guide.
General Hunting Area: Parkfield Valley.
Hunts Conducted On: Private land only, approximately 12,000 acres.
Months Hunting Available: All year around.
Hunting Methods Used: Spot & stalk, stands.
Weapons Allowed: Rifles; handguns.
Guide Fees: Meat Hog, $350; Trophy Boar, $550.
Trophy Boar Criteria: Two-inch tusks.
Do Guide Fees Include:
    Field dressing of game? Yes
    Hunt transportation? Yes
    Any food or drinks? No
Do You Also Offer?
    Place to sleep? Yes
    Meat locker facilities? No
    Meals/drinks? No
    Camping in tents, trailers, RV's? Yes
    Transport head to taxidermist? Yes
    Transport meat to butcher? No

Name: **Eldon Bergman, 3250 Vineyard Dr., Paso Robles, CA 93446.**
Phone: Day (805) 995-3093; Evening (805) 238-5504.
Years As Hog Guide? 37 years.
Hunters Guided Per Year? 90.
Approximate Success Rate? Meat Hog, 85%; Trophy Boar, 70%.
Maximum Number of Hunters/Trip? Four.
General Hunting Area? San Luis Obispo, southern Monterey counties.
Hunts Conducted On: Private land only, approximately 14,000 acres.
Months Hunting Available: All year.
Hunting Methods Used: Spot & stalk, stands, drives.
Weapons Allowed: Rifles; handguns; muzzleloaders; archery gear.
Guide Fees: Not available.
Trophy Boar Criteria: Not available.
Do Guide Fees Include:
    Field dressing of game? Yes
    Hunt transportation? Yes
    Any Food or Drinks? No
Do You Also Offer:
    Place to sleep? Yes
    Meat locker facilities? Yes
    Meals, drinks? No
    Camping in tents, trailers, RV's? No
    Transport head to taxidermist? Yes
    Transport meat to butcher? Yes

Name: Camp Five Outfitters, Craig Rossier, 1230 Arbor Rd., Paso Robles, CA 93446.
Phone: Day (805) 237-1201; Evening (805) 237-1201.
Years As Hog Guide: Eight years.
Hunters Guided Per Year: 300.
Approximate Success Rate: Meat hog, 98%; Trophy boar, 50%.
Maximum Number of Hunters/Trip: Three (one to three per guide.)
General Hunting Area: Southern Monterey County.
Hunts Conducted On: Private land only, approximately 9000 acres.
Months Hunting Available: All year.
Hunting Methods Used: Spot & stalk; stands; drives.
Weapons Allowed: Rifles; handguns; muzzleloaders; archery gear.
Guide Fees: Meat hog, $450; Trophy boar, $650.
Trophy boar Criteria: Not available.
Do Guide Fees Include:
> Field Dressing of Game? Yes
> Hunt transportation? Yes
> Any food or drinks? No
Do You Also Offer:
> Place to sleep? Yes, extra charge
> Meat locker facilities? Yes
> Meals/drinks? Yes, extra charge
> Camping in tents/trailers/RV's? Yes
> Transport of head to taxidermist? Yes
> Transport meat to butcher? Yes

**Name: Craig's Guide Service, Craig Van Housen, 6475 Jacobsen Rd.,
Kelseyville, CA 95451.**
Phone: Day (707) 279-0422; Evening (707) 279-0422.
Years As Hog Guide: 10 years.
Hunters Guided Per Year: 30.
Approximate Success Rate: Meat hogs, 95%; Trophy boar, 35%.
Maximum Number of Hunters/Trip: Two on dog hunts; three on spot & stalk hunts.
General Hunting Area: Mendocino County (Boonville/Ukiah area.)
Hunts Conducted On: Private land only, approximately 8200 acres.
Months Hunting Available: October-May.
Hunting Methods Used: Spot & Stalk; Dogs.
Weapons Allowed: Rifles; handguns.
Guide Fees: Meat hog, $100/day, $225 kill fee; Trophy boar, same.
Trophy Boar Criteria: two-inch tusks.
Do Guide Fees Include:
> Field dressing of game? Yes
> Hunt transportation? Yes
> Any food or drinks? No
Do You Also Offer:
> Place to sleep? No
> Meat locker facilities? Yes
> Meals/drinks? No
> Camping in tents/trailers/RV's? Yes
> Transport of head to taxidermist? Yes
> Transport of meat to butcher? Yes

Name: **Dye Creek Preserve, P.O. Box 1210, West Point, CA 95255.**
Phone: Day (209) 293-7087; Evening (209) 293-7087.
Years As Hog Guides: 25 years.
Hunters Guided Per Year: 100-150.
Approximate Success Rate: Meat hog, 98%; Trophy boar, 80%.
Maximum Number of Hunters/Trip? Six (two hunters/one guide.)
General Hunting Area: Dye Creek Ranch, near Red Bluff.
Hunts Conducted On: Private land only, 37,000 acres.
Months Hunting Available: December-April.
Hunting Methods Used: Spot & stalk, drives.
Weapons Allowed: Rifles; handguns; muzzleloaders; archery gear.
Guide Fees: Meat hogs, $550/two days; Trophy boar, $750.
Trophy Boar Criteria: two-inch tusks.
Do Guide Fees Include:
      Field dressing of game? Yes
      Hunt transportation? Yes
      Any food or drinks? Yes
Do You Also Offer:
      Place to sleep? Yes
      Meat locker facilities? Yes
      Camping in tents/trailers/RV's? No
      Meals/drinks? Yes
      Transport head to taxidermist? Yes
      Transport meat to butcher? Yes

Name: **Eastwood Guide Service, P.O. Box 1865, King City, CA 93930.**
Phone: Day (408) 385-3667; Evening (408) 385-3667.
Years As Hog Guide: 10 years.
Hunters Guided Per Year? N/A.
Approximate Success Rate? Meat hog, 100%; Trophy boar, N/A.
Maximum Number of Hunters/Trip? Five.
General Hunting Area: Monterey, San Benito counties.
Hunts Conducted On: Private land only, approximately 30,000 acres.
Months Hunting Available: All year.
Hunting Methods Used: Spot & stalk, stands, dogs.
Weapons Allowed: Rifles; handguns; muzzleloaders; archery gear.
Guide Fees: Meat hog, $300; Trophy boar, $300.
Trophy Boar Criteria: Don't book trophy hunts.
Do Guide Fees Include:
      Field dressing of game? Yes
      Hunt transportation? Yes
      Any food or drinks? No
Do You Also Offer:
      Place to sleep? No
      Meat locker facilities? Yes
      Camping in tents/trailers/RV's? No
      Transportation of head to taxidermist? Yes
      Transportation of meat to butcher? Yes

Name: **Scott Galloway, 3557 Piner Rd., Santa Rosa, CA 95401.**
Phone: Day (707) 545-7049; Evening (707) 545-7049.
Years As Hog Guide: 10 years.
Hunters Guided Per Year? 30-50.
Approximate Success Rate: Meat hog, 100%; Trophy boar, 20%.
Maximum Number of Hunters/Trip? Four (two hunters/one guide).
General Hunting Area: Sonoma, Mendocino county foothills.
Hunts Conducted On: Private land only, approximately 4000 acres.
Months Hunting Available: November-May.
Hunting Methods Used: Spot & stalk; Dogs.
Weapons Allowed: Rifles; handguns; muzzleloaders; archery gear.
Guide Fees: Meat hog, $275 to $350; Trophy boar, $275 to $350.
Trophy Boar Criteria: Two-inch tusks.
Do Guide Fees Include:
    Field dressing of game? Yes
    Hunt transportation? Yes
    Any Food or drinks? Yes
Do You Also Offer:
    Place to sleep? No
    Meat locker facilities? No
    Meals/drinks? Yes
    Camping in tents/trailers/RV's? Yes
    Transport head to taxidermist? Yes
    Transport meat to butcher? Yes

Name: **Don Ingalls, 53100 Pine Canyon Rd., King City, CA 93930.**
Phone: Day (408) 385-3754; Evening (408) 385-3754.
Years As Hog Guide: 23 years.
Hunters Guided Per Year: 200.
Approximate Success Rate: Meat hog, 90%; Trophy boar, 90%.
Maximum Number of Hunters/Trip? Eight (two hunters/one guide.)
General Hunting Area: Monterey County.
Hunts Conducted On: Private land, approximately 43,000 acres.
Months Hunting Available: All year.
Hunting Methods Used: Spot & stalk, dogs.
Weapons Allowed: Rifles; handguns; muzzleloaders; archery gear.
Guide Fees: Meat hog, $675; Trophy boar: $675.
Trophy Boar Criteria: Three-inch tusks.
Do Guide Fees Include:
    Field dressing of game: Yes
    Hunt transportation? Yes
    Any food or drinks? Yes
Do You Also Offer:
    Place to sleep? Yes
    Meat locker facilities? Yes
    Meals/drinks? Yes, included in guide fees
    Camping in tents/trailers/RV's? Yes
    Transport of head to taxidermist? Yes
    Transport of meat to butcher? No

Name: **Las Viboras Wild Boar Hunts, 5420 Comstock Rd., Hollister, CA 95023.**
Phone: Day (408) 637-7770; Evening (408) 637-7770.
Years As Hog Guide: 10 years,
Hunters Guided Per Year: 25 to 30.
Approximate Success Rate: Meat hog, 95%; Trophy boar, N/A.
Maximum Number of Hunters/Trip? One on one hunts only.
General Hunting Area: San Benito County, near Hollister.
Hunts Conducted On: Private land only, approximately 7200 acres.
Months Hunting Available: October-May.
Hunting Methods Used: Spot & stalk, dogs.
Weapons Allowed: Rifles; handguns; muzzleloaders.
Guide Fees: Not available.
Trophy Boar Criteria: N/A.
Do Guide Fees Include:
    Field dressing of game? Yes
    Hunt transportation? Yes
    Any food or drinks? Yes
Do You Also Offer:
    Place to sleep? No
    Meat locker facilities? No
    Meals/drinks? Yes
    Transport of head to taxidermist? Yes
    Transport of meat to butcher? No

Name: **Silva's Guide Service, 14487 L.G. Almaden Rd., Los Gatos, CA 95030.**
Phone: Day (408) 723-8759; Evening (408) 723-8759.
Years As Hog Guide: 10 years.
Hunters Guided Per Year: 35.
Approximate Success Rate? Meat hog, 90%; Trophy boar, 60%.
Maximum Number of Hunters/Trip: Two.
General Hunting Area: Central California.
Hunts Conducted On: Private land, approximately 100,000 acres.
Months Hunting Available: October-May.
Hunting Methods Used: Dogs.
Weapons Allowed: Rifles; handguns.
Guide Fees: Meat hog, $350; Trophy boar, $550.
Trophy Boar Criteria: Two-inch tusks.
Do Guide Fees Include:
    Field dressing of game? Yes
    Hunt transportation? No
    Any food or drinks? No
Do You Also Offer:
    Place to sleep? No
    Meat locker facilities? No
    Meals/drinks? No
    Camping in tents/trailers/RV's? No
    Transport of head to taxidermist? No
    Transport of meat to butcher? No

Name: **Sonoma & Mendocino Wild Pig Hunts, Mitch Thorsen, 2995 Arden Way, Santa Rosa, CA 95403.**
Phone: Day (707) 579-7622; Evening (707) 576-4253.
Years As Hog Guides: 12 years.
Hunters Guided Per Year: 50 to 75.
Approximate Success Rate: Meat hog, 35%; Trophy boar, 65%.
Maximum Number of Hunters/Trip: Four (two hunters/one guide.)
General Hunting Area: Sonoma, Mendocino counties.
Hunts Conducted On: Private land only, approximately 17,400 acres.
Months Hunting Available: November-May.
Hunting Methods Used: Spot & stalk, dogs.
Weapons Allowed: Rifles, muzzleloaders.
Guide Fees: Meat hog, $500; Trophy boar, $500.
Trophy Boar Criteria: Two-inch tusks.
Do Guide Fees Include:
    Field dressing of game? Yes
    Hunt transportation? Yes
    Any food or drinks? Yes
Do You Also Offer:
    Place to sleep? Yes
    Meat locker facilities? Yes
    Meals/drinks? Yes, included in hunt cost
    Camping in tents/trailers/RV's? Yes
    Transport of head to taxidermist? Yes, $25
    Transport of meat to butcher? Yes, $25

Name: **Ed Sparling, 5420 Comstock Rd., Hollister, CA 95023.**
Phone: Day (408) 637-7770; Evening (408) 637-7770.
Years As Hog Guide: 9 years.
Hunters Guided Per Year: 40.
Approximate Success Rate: Meat hog, 90%; Trophy boar, n/a.
Maximum Number of Hunters/Trip? Two (two hunters/one guide.)
General Hunting Area: San Benito County.
Hunts Conducted On: Private land only, approximately 7400 acres.
Months Hunting Available: November-April.
Hunting Methods Used: Dogs.
Weapons Allowed: Rifle; handgun; muzzleloader.
Guide Fees: $300, all hogs.
Trophy Boar Criteria: n/a.
Do Your Guide Fees Include:
    Field dressing of game? Yes
    Hunt Transportation? Yes
    Any food/drink? Yes
Do You Also Offer:
    Place to sleep? No
    Meat Locker Facilities? No
    Meals, drinks? Yes
    Camping in tents/trailers/RV's? No
    Transport head to taxidermist? Yes
    Transport meat to butcher? No

Name: **Tim Vadon, 200 N. Wash St., Cloverdale, CA 95425.**
Phone: Day (707) 894-2900; Evening (707) 894-2900.
Years As Hog Guide: 10
Hunters Guided Per Year: 15-25.
Approximate Success Rate: Meat hog, 80%; Trophy boar, 15%.
Maximum Number of Hunters/Trip: Four (two hunters/one guide.)
General Hunting Area: Mendocino County, near Yorkville.
Hunts Conducted On: Private land only, approximately 3000 acres.
Months Hunting Available: November through April.
Hunting Methods Used: Drives; dogs; stands.
Weapons Allowed: Rifle, muzzleloader.
Guide Fees: Meat hog, $250; Trophy boar, $300.
Trophy Boar Criteria: 150 pounds & over.
Do Guide Fees Include:
    Hunt transportation? Yes
    Field dressing of game? Yes
    Any food or drink? No
Do You Also Offer:
    Place to sleep? No
    Meat locker facilities? Yes
    Meals/drinks? No
    Camping in Tents/trailers/RV's? No
    Transport head to taxidermist? Yes
    Transport meat to butcher? No

Name: **Wilderness Unlimited, Rick Copeland, 27575 Industrial Blvd.,
Hayward, CA 94545**
Phone: Day (510) 785-4868; Evening (510) 785-4868.
Years As Hog Guide: n/a.
Hunters Per Year: Approximately 300.
Approximate Success Rate: 20% (all pigs.)
Maximum Number of Hunters/Trip: Varies.
General Hunting Area: Mendocino/Monterey counties.
Hunts Conducted On: Private land only, approximately 46,000 acres.
Months Hunting Available: April-May; July-January.
Hunting Methods Used: Spot & stalk; drives; stands (no dogs permitted.)
Weapons Allowed: Rifles; handguns; muzzleloaders; archery gear.
Guide Fees: None (club membership required.)
Author's Note: Wilderness Unlimited is a club program, whereby members are allowed to hunt a wide variety of different ranches on which WU has leased the hunting/fishing rights on throughout the state, in accordance with to club rules and regulations. Some of their properties have very good wild boar hunting available. Call or write them for their latest brochure and more information on their innovative program.

Name: **Wild Pig Hunting, Inc., Ken Whittaker, P.O. Box 60, Yorkville,** CA 95494.
Phone: Day (707) 894-3280; Evening (707) 894-3280.
Years As Hog Guide: 20
Hunters Guided Per Year: 700
Approximate Success Rate: Guided hunts, 95%; Unguided spot & stalk hunts, 35%.
Maximum Number of Hunters/Trip: Guided, 3-4; Unguided, 3 to 12.
General Hunting Area: Sonoma County, near Cloverdale.
Hunts Conducted On: Private land only, approximately 700 acres.
Hunting Methods Used: Spot & stalk; dogs.
Weapons Allowed: Rifles; handguns; muzzleloaders; archery gear.
Guide Fees: Guided meat or trophy boar, $350; Unguided spot & stalk, meat hog or trophy boar, $150/one day, $275/two days.
Trophy Boar Criteria: n/a.
Do Guide Fees Include:
    Field dressing of game? Yes
    Hunt transportation? Yes
    Any food or drinks? No
Do You Also Offer:
    Place to sleep? No
    Meat locker facilities? No
    Meals/drinks? No
    Camping in tents/trailers/RV's? Yes
    Transport of head to taxidermist? No
    Transport of meat to butcher? No

Name: **Williamson Brothers Ranch, 288 Echo Valley Rd., Salinas, CA 93907.**
Phone: Day (408) 663-4980; Evening (408) 663-4980.
Years As Hog Guide: 18 years.
Hunters Guided Per Year: Not available.
Approximate Success Rate: Meat hog, 90%; Trophy boar, 60%.
Maximum Number of Hunters/Trip: Three.
General Hunting Area: Monterey County.
Hunts Conducted On: Private land only, approximately 3000 acres.
Months Hunting Available: All year.
Hunting Methods Used: Dogs.
Weapons Allowed: Rifles; handguns; muzzleloaders; archery gear.
Guide Fees: Meat hog, $350; Trophy boar, $550.
Trophy Boar Criteria: 200 pounds.
Do Guide Fees Include:
    Field dressing of game? Yes
    Hunt transportation? Yes
    Any food or drinks? No
Do You Also Offer:
    Place to sleep? Yes
    Meat locker facilities? No
    Meals/drinks? Yes, at extra cost
    Transport of head to taxidermist? Yes
    Transport of meat to butcher shop? No

Name: **Tom Willoughby, P.O. Box 1466, King City, CA 93930.**
Phone: Day (408) 385-3003; Evening (408) 385-3003.
Years As Hog Guide: 12 years.
Hunters Guided Per Year: n/a.
Approximate Success Rate: 98% overall.
Maximum Number of Hunters/Trip: Eight (three hunters/one guide.)
General Hunting Area: Monterey County.
Hunts Conducted On: Private land only, approximately 100,000 acres.
Months Hunting Available: All year.
Hunting Methods Used: Spot & stalk; dogs.
Weapons Allowed: Rifles.
Guide Fees: Meat hog, $475; Trophy boar, $750.
Trophy Boar Criteria: Two-inch tusks.
Do Guide Fees Include:
　　Field dressing of game? Yes
　　Hunt transportation? Yes
　　Any food or drink? No
Do You Also Offer:
　　Place to sleep? No
　　Meat locker facilities? Yes
　　Camping in tents/trailers/RV's? Yes
　　Transport head to taxidermist? Yes
　　Transport meat to butcher? No

Name: **Work's Wildlife Management, Burt & Kris Claussen, Star Rte., Box 4640, San Miguel, CA 93451.**
Phone: Day (805) 467-3262; Evening (805) 467-3262.
Years As Hog Guide? 15 years.
Hunters Guided Per Year: 300.
Approximate Success Rate: Meat hog, 60%; Trophy Boar, 60%.
Maximum Number of Hunters/Trip: Eight (two hunters/guide).
General Hunting Area: Parkfield Valley.
Hunts Conducted On: Private land only, approximately 12,000 acres.
Months Hunting Available: All year.
Hunting Methods Used: Spot & stalk, drives.
Weapons Allowed: Rifles; handguns; muzzleloaders; archery gear.
Guide Fees: Meat hog, $275, plus $150 kill fee; Trophy Boar, $275, plus $250 kill fee.
Trophy Boar Criteria: Two-inch tusks.
Do Guide Fees Include:
　　Field dressing of Game? Yes
　　Hunt transportation? Yes
　　Any food or drinks? Yes
Do you Also Offer:
　　Place to sleep? Yes, no extra cost
　　Meat locker facilities? Yes
　　Meals/drinks? Yes, no extra cost
　　Transport of head to taxidermist? Yes
　　Transport of meat to butcher? Yes

THE "BOSS HAWG" WILD BOAR CALL

Shortly after "Hunting Wild Boar In California" was written, Bob Robb began working with Eli Haydel of Haydel's Game Calls, and helped develop the "Boss Hawg" wild boar call. Wild boar are very fraternal animals, as well as very vocal. They like to talk to each other, and can be heard snuffling and grunting all day long. This call imitates the fraternal sound wild hogs make as they feed along together. By blowing louder, the loud squall made by a large boar can be imitated. Bob has called up and shot nearly two dozen hogs with this call, many of them with his bow. In addition, the call will help settle down any hogs that may have seen or heard, but not smelled, you. It's excellent for use in thick brush. Complete with instructions.

Video: HUNTING WILD BOAR

Filmed entirely in California, this action-packed video is chock full of hunting tips, close-up footage of wild boar and other wildlife, and much more. Bob Robb, Larry Jones, and John Higley harvest three good boars on camera, two with bows and one with a muzzleloader. Along the way, they show you important keys to successfully hunting hogs, including locating, calling, stalking, and ambushing them, as well as what hogs eat, where they bed, water, etc. One hour long, and edited for family viewing. Produced by Wilderness Sound Productions.

Please send me _____ "Boss Hawg" wild boar calls. Enclosed is $14.95 for each call, plus $2.00 shipping and handling per call.

Please send me _____ "Hunting Wild Boar" videos. Enclosed is $24.95 for each video, plus $2.00 shipping and handling per video.

NAME _____

ADDRESS _____

CITY _____ STATE _____ ZIP _____

I unerstand it will take three weeks for delivery.

Mail to: Bob Robb
P.O. Box 1296
Valdez, AK 99686

ELK HUNTING WITH THE EXPERTS

The most complete, up-to-date book on hunting North American elk available today. The 176-page, 6x9 soft-cover book features 16 chapters, 80 photographs and charts, and 3 appendixes that cover both how to hunt elk with firearms and archery gear, as well as surveys all the states in the lower 48 that permit elk hunting, as well as Canada and Alaska, to tell you where the best elk hunting can be found on the continent today. In addition, well-known elk hunting experts like Jim Zumbo, Craig Boddington, Larry D. Jones, Jack Atcheson, and others share their secrets for successfully hunting elk during all seasons in individual chapters. That, together with Bob Robb's elk hunting experience that spans more than 15 years and includes hunts in all western states except two, plus Canada and Alaska, combines to give you a complete look at both our elk, and elk hunting. Whether you want to hunt elk on your own out of a backpack or from your vehicle, or are interested in a guided adventure, this is an invaluable reference source.

Please send me _____ autographed copies of "Elk Hunting With The Experts." Enclosed is $16.95, plus $2.50 postage and handling for each book ordered. Please send my book(s) to:

NAME _____

ADDRESS _____

CITY _____ STATE _____ ZIP _____

I understand it will take three weeks for delivery.

Mail to: Bob Robb
                     P.O. Box 1296
                     Valdez, AK 99686

DEER HUNTING COAST TO COAST

Bob Robb and Craig Boddington, Editor of Petersen's HUNT-ING magazine, have recently written the most comprehensive, up-to-date book on deer hunting in North America. "Deer Hunting Coast To Coast" is a hardcover book published by Safari Press that contains over 250 pages and 125 photographs, and discusses in detail all aspects of deer hunting. Included are chapters on where to find today's best hunting areas for trophy-class mule deer, whitetails, blacktails, and Coues deer; the best guns and loads for deer hunting under a variety of conditions and locations; how to best hunt deer in the east, west, north, and south; how to book hunts in Canada and Mexico; tips on equipment; how to glass; and much, much more. The book is filled with exciting hunting stories, too, and written by two of the country's best-known hunting writers, men who both have been hunting deer from coast to coast for over 25 years.

Please send me _____ autographed copies of "Deer Hunting Coast To Coast." Enclosed is $22.95 plus $2.50 postage and handling for each book ordered (California residents add $1.50 sales tax per book ordered). Please send my book(s) to:

NAME _____

ADDRESS _____

CITY _____ STATE _____ ZIP _____

I understand it will take three weeks for delivery.

Mail to: **Bob Robb**
P.O. Box 1296
Valdez, AK 99686

CONVENIENT ORDER FORM

I would like to order more copies of this book at $14.95 (postpaid). Discount 10% if ordering two or three books. Discount 20% if ordering four or more books. Please allow three weeks for delivery. Thanks.

NAME_____

ADDRESS_____

CITY_____STATE_____ZIP_____

Number of books being ordered_____

TOTAL AMOUNT ENCLOSED
(Check or Money Order) $_____

Mail to: **Bob Robb**
             P.O. Box 1296
             Valdez, AK 99686

Larsen's Outdoor Publishing also publishes the "Bass Series Library," eight books on various aspects of catching largemouth bass. For more information, write Larsen's Outdoor Publishing, Dept. "ROBB", 2640 Elizabeth Place, Lakeland, FL 33813.